"If your dog doesn't like this book,
he has no sense of humor."
—*Roy Blount, Jr.*

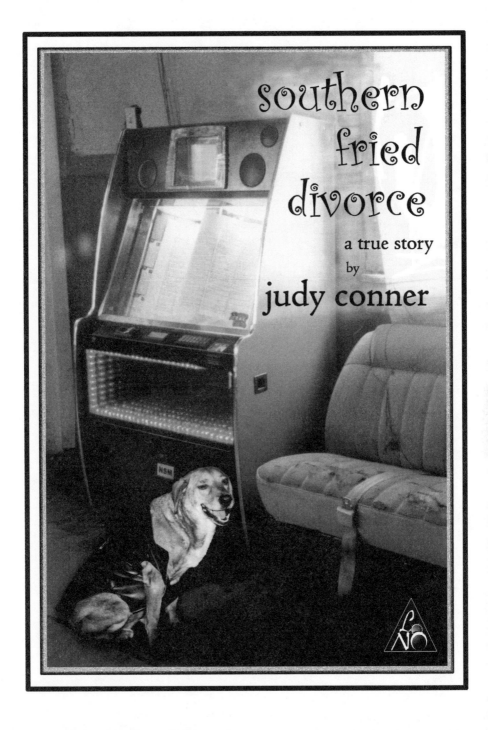

southern
fried
divorce

a true story

by

judy conner

818,602
Con

Copyright © 2004 by Judy Conner

Cover and Book Design by Joshua Clark
Front cover painting by Vidho Lorvillle (www.vidholorville.com)
Photography by Joshua Clark

Light of New Orleans Publishing, LLC
828 Royal Street #307
New Orleans, Louisiana 70116

www.southernfrieddivorce.com

Publisher's Cataloging-in-Publication Data *(Provided by Quality Books, Inc.)*

Conner, Judy.
    Southern fried divorce / Judy Conner.
    p. cm.
    LCCN 2003114228
    ISBN 0-9714076-8-1

    1.   Marriage—Humor. 2. Divorce—Humor 3. New
Orleans (La.)—Humor. 4. Love—Humor. 5. Dogs—Humor.
6. Southern states—Social life and customs—Humor.
7. American wit and humor. I. Title.

PN6165.C66 2004   818'.602
                                   QBI33-1671

to Trevor

TUNA AND THE WOMAN

I don't know what got into me.
I think it may have been an insect of communist persuasion,
but that's just good ole Tchoupitoulas Street conjecture.
Coming home early from work one day,
what I found was my loving wife
having an affair with a tuna.
No love of my life
and no tunafish sandwich.
How cruel can one life be?
The Friends of Seaworld sticker on her car
became a harbinger of symbolism,
as if Melville were somewhere in paradise
writing the script of my life.
I removed the aquarium of course.
When I gave her fishsticks for Christmas
I think she became suspicious,
but, when I gave her fishing tackle for Easter
I'm sure she suspected
I knew.

—Chris Champagne

southern
fried
divorce

Christmas Memories

NOT LONG AFTER I BECAME HIS EX-WIFE, that ex-husband brought me a .38 blue steel revolver and a brown fuzzy puppy. His unannounced arrival at my new bachelorette maisonette was not a complete surprise. He'd always been fond of barging in where not invited. So I didn't really expect him to stand on ceremony and wait for an invitation that might be delayed indefinitely.

I barely heard the doorbell over the sound of the Carrollton Avenue streetcar as it passed, headed for the nearby car barn to be watered and fed. I opened the door of my shotgun double apartment to greet my former mate, beaming with good will and Jim Beam. He was festooned with red and green ribbon and carrying a couple of intriguing items. Belated Christmas offerings, I guessed, since we were pretty deep into spring.

"Surprise!" he bellowed. "And seasonable greetings! Here, I've brought you a new home security package. You can learn how to shoot this gun and this puppy'll grow up to be a fine watch dog. Lookit how he's watching you right now."

"Well, how thoughtful," I murmured.

After his fifteen years of quasi-husbanding, I guess he was finding it hard to quit at least musing on my welfare. Crime in New Orleans at the time was common as mildew. Just part of the landscape. One of the downsides to the endearing openness of the locals is that they might open your door as readily as they open their own. What's yours is theirs. They just don't have well-defined boundaries.

I toyed with the five bullets that accompanied the gun and wondered what kind of fool gives his ex-wife a gun. Especially one who sometimes has the disposition of a wolverine. And why'd he get only five bullets for a six-shooter? Perhaps for a game of Redneck Roulette? It's similar to Russian Roulette, just a whole lot more daring. Your average redneck will rarely resist a dare. That probably helps account for their historically out-of-proportion representation in the wartime military. They've always figured prominently in the body counts too.

For Russian Roulette, they use one bullet and five empty chambers—because of the Russian economy. Shortages of everything but vodka, so I hear. The Redneck version is just the reverse—five bullets, one empty chamber. Much more efficient.

Anyhow, a gun was not something I'd have chosen for myself. However, I didn't already have one and this one appeared to be a nice, sturdy model and not at all cheap. It's the thought that counts.

"What made you think to get me a dog?" I asked him.

Now that ex-husband got all fired-up. "It was just pitiful," he said. "I was over by Franky and Johnny's picking up some hot crawfish when I saw a bunch of kids there on Tchoupitoulas Street. When I drove closer, I saw that they had a hold of this puppy's arms and legs. They were teasing him and pulling on him. I just whipped my car off to the side and jumped out and starting hollering and slinging kids. I snatched this puppy and took off. As I was driving along, of course, I thought of you and how you just love puppies."

It was, of course, true that I love puppies. And pie. And mother and the flag. And assorted strays of all kinds.

My glance shifted from the puppy to the broad, usually guileless face of that ex-husband. The innocent look was gone, replaced by that other one. He lied about stuff that didn't matter at all as regularly as he did about stuff to save his hide. He was a sport-liar and a real enthusiast of writer Dan Jenkins' "Are you going to believe me or your lyin' eyes?" And to a lesser degree, "That's my story and I'm stickin' to it!"

"What's the real deal on the dog?" I snapped.

"Well, I was over at Joey K's eating a shrimp po'boy with Clay. You know Clay is the guy who bought Joey K's from Joey K."

"Yes, I know that, I go there all the time. What does that have to do with this dog?" I wondered if very many people lie about their lunch.

"Joey K was in there, too, eating a po'boy with Clay. And having a beer in one of those big ole heavy, iced tea glasses Clay uses. Joey K's brown dog, Betty, was there, and her puppies—just the right size for giving away. As you can see," he answered.

I could see a light brown fuzz ball about the size of a cantaloupe with dark eyes and nose and eyebrows. Mighty cute. How many ugly puppies have you seen? I'm pretty sure there are way more ugly babies. If this one took after his mother, Betty, he'd grow up to be a medium-sized, medium-haired, medium-eared, medium-brown, medium-hound-type dog. Generic dog. But the eyebrows were a redeeming factor. I purely love a dog with eyebrows.

So, I bedded the critter down in the laundry room at the very back of the shotgun—as far from the bedrooms as possible. I was hoping that the pup would let me and my new housemate get some sleep.

I had lately opened my heart and my hearth to that ex-husband's nephew. I could not do otherwise. Whenever I got ready to fly that ex-husband's coop, that nephew said, "You're not going off and leaving me here by myself with my crazy uncle." I didn't mind. I was used to the teenager. He'd been with us for several years—ever since his mother had run off and joined the circus or the itinerant preachers or something. I forget. But the nephew was pretty different from both his mother and his uncle who acted like they'd been raised by wild dogs. He was just as sweet and smart and talented as could be. He showed a very early flair for the dramatic. During a visit to our house, he came into my bedroom as I was blabbing away on the phone. Three-year-olds can't stand for you to get on the phone or in the bathtub. I was barely aware of him there at the foot of the bed. I focused a bit and saw that he was gesturing mightily with three fingers of his right hand and madly raising his baby eyebrows up and down. "Three?" I mouthed at him. He nodded vigorously and began wildly bobbing and weaving. Then he raised his left hand behind him, lunged toward me flapping his right foot on the floor and pointing his right hand in a brilliant feint a la Errol Flynn. Abruptly, he stopped and again was stabbing the air with the three fingers. I got it, I got it! He wanted one of the Three Musketeer candy bars I'd squirreled away in the kitchen. Hiding things up high never worked; he could climb anything. But he never thought to stick his grimey paw into the cannister of dried red beans sitting innocently on the counter. I ended my phone call and gave his charade my full attention. He got a hearty "Bravo" and the candy bar.

Really, the only way he was like his family was that he was mighty messy. All them people were like pigs. We had an agreement whereby he'd keep his mess hemmed up in his room. So the common areas looked pretty good.

We had plenty of stuff because I had taken most of the furniture and every last knick-knack. I think I left that ex-husband the king-sized bed, the TV, the refrigerator, and an easy chair. To his credit, he had insisted that I take everything.

I wasn't too sure about this new puppy business. My confidence in my housebreaking abilities had been badly shaken by the failure of my marriage. I had put just about every scrap of energy I could muster into getting that husband to behave—with virtually no effect. Impervious. Based on my recent track record, I guessed I'd very shortly be knee deep in puppy poop. Although I guess if I wanted to, I could claim success at keeping that ex-husband from shitting on the floor. Of course, in a couple of weeks, my laundry room looked like the launching area for a school paper drive—lots and lots of nice clean newspaper. Not so the floor. That puppy had carefully, precisely shat betwixt the sheets of paper. I had scooped about four or five hundred piles of puppy poop off the floor and was past ready to quit.

I rang up that ex-husband and I said, "I love my new gun, but I'm fixing to take this brown dog to the pound."

Naturally, he came thundering over to intervene on the dog's behalf and call me names. "This is just plain heartless! You are the meanest woman in the world," he declared. "Not to mention ungrateful. This was a Christmas present!"

"Oh, it was not either. You just wanted to show off. And since you're so crazy about being the big hero, you can *just rescue this!*"

"I don't have *time* for a puppy."

"I don't either, but I do have time to take him to the SPCA!"

"*Well, dammit!*" he countered brilliantly.

"Yeah, dammit all," I declared. "You've got yourself a new brown dog!"

In fact, I had really done that ex-husband a favor. His night club business left his days pretty flexible. He could really use somebody to hang with since he was even harder on buddies than he was on wives. Just ask the one who had two loads of river sand show up on his front lawn. Just ask the one who got his picture taken—nekkid and tied to a bedstead by some slut in that ex-husband's "office." Just ask any one of a dozen or so who happened to be standing next to him when he took a notion to taunt bikers, seamen, drug dealers or other assorted thugs. And just ask the one who got tricked into carrying that ex-husband's bag through customs when they returned from a trip to Thailand. Yep, ask the guy how he felt when the inspector popped it open, and found nothing but pills, tablets, and capsules—thousands of them, just loose in there, full to the brim. It looked like somebody'd spent their entire vacation filling a suitcase with M&M's.

A puppy was just the kind of companion that ex-husband needed. The two became immediately inseparable. They'd set out together just about every day. They'd go to the hardware store and to the bank and to his nightclub business to harass the employees. He was in charge of the human resources part of the business. He also booked the nightly live music and took care of the endless bunch of crap that came with owning a club. Or any small business, for that matter. The advertising and marketing were my areas of expertise. After we split up, we continued the business partnership as before, except that I also started booking the music. I didn't want to but it was the only way I could get that ex-husband to readily agree to my full financial support. The real story was that he was damn sick and tired of booking music. He was always angling to do less of anything that did not directly pertain to plumbing or chasing nasty women. That man loved a broken or plugged-up toilet better than anything—even the nasty women. We had once talked about his becoming a plumber. My position was one of neutrality, but I had pointed out that it would be a shame for him to drop out of law school to become a plumber unless he was really committed to this vocation.

As it turned out, he was not really committed to pipes and drains and hairballs and such. It was just that he had discovered that he was uncommitted to and bored blind by the law. The study of it, that is. He had always had an aversion to obeying it. I believe he may still hold the record for "Drunk and Disorderlies" in his home area—the northwest section of the District of Columbia.

One fine day in New Orleans, he was yet again not in class. He wandered into a neighborhood bar on Lowerline Street. It was called the University Inn because it was near Tulane University. He fell in love with the place. Pretty soon he had convinced the owner, Bob, that a partner would be just the thing. Poor Bob. As soon as he could thereafter, he bought Bob out. Thus began his professional career in adult recreation. We both assumed that his extensive experience as an amateur would stand him in good stead.

We offered only draft beer, peanuts, and hilarity for a clientele consisting mostly of the neighborhood rabble plus Tulane students and faculty. But for such a hole-in-the-wall, it did well. And it was big fun. It was mighty convenient for that ex-husband. He had found an occupation where he could pretty much be a shiftless ne'er-do-well right there on the job.

Just about the time his lease on the space was running out, he had saved up some money. With the help of one of his faithful customers, Matt Gregory, he was able to buy a building and open a new and improved fun spot.

Matt was the first native New Orleanian who was willing to be our friend. And it took us two years to get him. As a matter of fact, I was wondering if we'd ever get one. It was so weird because I'd been pretty popular in college and that ex-husband had always had a bunch of friends, albethey motley. We even discussed the possibility that we might, in fact, be a pair of losers. What if, during those years of prancing around all biggety-speckle, thinking we were mighty cute and pretty cool, we were actually kinda creepy. But, no, that couldn't be it.

We finally did figure out why it was so hard to make friends among the natives. It's because most of the people who are born here never leave and if they do they spend the rest of their lives trying to get back. And most of 'em are Catholic, tending to larger families. So everyone you meet has friends going back to kindergarten plus cousins ahoy. In fact, right from the start, children are encouraged to be best friends with their cousins. Isn't that strange? It's like they're all in the Mafia or something. Even when they give big parties, their guest lists are just about filled up with family. These folks do not get to do hardly anything without the whole damn family. They just plain don't have time in their lives for anybody new. You've just got to be real patient til they can fit you in. It is true, though, that once they do make a place for you in their lives, it's pretty hard to get yourself kicked out.

For instance—Matt Gregory—guess what we did to him? I have to say "we" because this was one of the few times where I was involved in some nefarious activity with that ex-husband. At the time, Matt was married to his first wife. He was also carrying on an extra-marital affair of which we did not approve. Naturally, I didn't approve, but I thought it pretty fascinating that that ex-husband didn't either. Even I knew this was a really black pot calling names. Fairness notwithstanding, that ex-husband was extremely vocal in his criticism of Matt and his "Nymphet" as we had christened the hapless honey. He even barred the twosome from the tavern. Although Matt was welcomed solo. There came the time that we knew in advance that Matt would be out of town. He was going to New York for a week on business. He had been foolish enough to divulge that the "Nymphet" would be meeting him there. This plan really annoyed that ex-husband and he ranted about it quite a bit. We kicked it around and finally, between us, developed a plan. We wrote a press release for a newspaper column dedicated to the doings of locals. We sent it in and it was printed.

> Attorney Matt Gregory will be jetting to New York for the KNOBGLOBBEN SUGAR FESTIVAL and will be enjoying same for the better part of next week.

Oh, by the way, "Sugar" was the nymphet's name.

That ex-husband was kind enough to warn him that something might be in the paper sometime. Poor Matt had to get up at dawn:thirty every day for weeks to snag the paper before his wife got up.

Now, even after that, Matt helped us purchase the property that would house the next bigger and better night club.

The new establishment was located on Oak Street, in the heart of the Carrollton area. The Mardi Gras parade put on by the Krewe of Carrollton used to roll on Oak Street. The route was changed because one year there was a real high wind that blew a krewe member off the float when it was on an overpass. It was very bad. The new plan excluded Oak Street. I think that marked the beginning of the street's eventual decline as a center of commerce.

The brown dog and that ex-husband spent so much time together that after a while there came to be a family resemblance between them. I once remarked to that ex-husband that the brown dog looked quite a bit like his cousin—one of the ones who'd run off to join the circus or pick fruit or something. I forget. She had a long, thin brown face and brown eyes. Just like the brown dog. That ex-husband's face was brown year-round also and he had the brown eyes. But he had a very big face. Taking up more than 50% of his head and kind of squarish. So he and the dog didn't look so much alike except through the eyes. That ex-husband replied snappishly that the dog was still a teenager and would surely outgrow the resemblance to the cousin.

Very big faces run in my family, too. Along with some pretty big butts. Big tits do not run in my family. However, I was blessed as a mutant in that department. I can assure you that big tits never go out of style. If we could just get it where big butts are popular life would be perfect.

I guess the brown dog had been with that ex-husband about a year when I began the custom of the **Christmas Roast**. I fixed it the same way every year and the brown dog liked it very, very much. It went thusly:

Take a 5 or 6 pound roast—I would choose a sirloin tip, but you could use a cheaper cut if you're the stingy type. In my own case, it's pretty much "Nothin's too good for this dog."

Preheat oven to 500 degrees—yep, that's 500 degrees. Hot. Mix together 4 teaspoons of salt, 2 teaspoons of cayenne pepper, 2 teaspoons of coarse ground black pepper. Smear this mixture all over the roast. Cook uncovered in a dutch oven or big iron skillet for 7 minutes per pound. Turn the oven off and DO NOT OPEN THE OVEN DOOR. Do not open the door right from the start and not for at least an hour and a half after you turn the oven off. You will be tempted to peep in and out of there, but DON'T DO IT—it will mess it up if you do. If you cannot follow these di-

rections, cook your roast some other way. When the time is up, remove and let stand for 10 minutes.

For people: slice and serve. For brown dogs: cut off the spicy crust. This roast will be rare. You can cook longer per pound if your dog prefers medium or well-done.

When I fix this roast for people, I also make these killer *mashed potatoes*—even though there will not be a whole lot of gravy.

White or red taters will do. Peel, slice, cover with water in pretty heavy pot. Bring to boil, then simmer til done. Drain in colander and dump taters back in the pot. Add lots of butter, some salt and white pepper to taste. Do not substitute black pepper, it's not the same. Pour in a dab of whipping cream and mash it all together. Then whisk, adding cream as needed, til you get the texture you like. I like some lumps myself. Good as ice cream.

The brown dog would come to sleep over at my house so he'd have time to eat all of the roast. It was hard, but he persevered. I'd serve him the first portion for early dinner, around 5 in the afternoon. He'd feed intermittently throughout the evening and finish up about 2 AM. Then he would go fast asleep with all four legs straight up in the air, which would soon be thick with brown dog gas. Sometimes he'd fart so loud that he'd wake himself up. Then he would look around suspiciously, growling softly for good measure. He'd give a big yawn—tasting it—smack, smack, smack—and nod back off.

The reason I cooked a whole roast for the brown dog was because, even though I'd given him to that ex-husband, I wanted the dog to like me best. It was a common desire of mine. I might not be the only one, but I would, by God, be number one.

I am pleased to report that my Christmas roast was his favorite present and the brown dog looked forward to the consumption with glee. You could readily tell this because the only time he broke out of a shuffle was from the car to my front door for that Christmas roast. He generally liked to move as slowly as possible to annoy that ex-husband. The brown dog would usually stall around in the car, yawning and stretching, until he'd been invited to disembark at least three or four times. And even then he'd move like a thousand-year-old dog. Well, on Christmas Roast Night, he'd bound from that car before it was stopped good, and his nails on the sidewalk would be shootin' sparks. You're probably wondering how he knew Roast Night from any other. Well, he was always a great one for skulking around and eavesdropping. Sometimes I would manage to surprise him. I'd phone up that ex-husband and tell him, "Now don't say anything, just listen. I don't want the brown dog to know, so bring him over for the roast two days before Christmas."

One time that ex-husband brought along a friend, besides the brown dog, for the roast. It was this guy from Ireland who, by the way, was on a list of the ten most eligible bachelors in all of Ireland. Since he had this actual credential, I was, at first, pleased when he pronounced me a winsome lass, even though I was pretty sure that the top scorer would be the toothsome wench. This was a most charming Irishman, but his general attitude regarding the consumption of spirits and well, work, would clearly make him ineligible for any list of marriageable guys that I would compile. I think that country might have had more problems than bad food, bad teeth, and a history of crop failure. I think it is so great that the Irish have turned their country around so nicely.

Mr. Ireland was not my only foreign encounter that day. Earlier, I'd been to a holiday reception at the International Trade Mart. I was greeted by a very charming Latin gentlemen. He smiled, bowed slightly over my hand and said, "Feliz Navidad." I replied happily, "So nice to meet you, Feliz." After meeting half a dozen or so funseekers, all named Feliz, I figured it out: Feliz is Spanish for "Dude."

Anyway, that ex-husband and his Irish buddy decided to stay for the consumption. They were shortly joined by that ex-husband's nephew, who loved celebrations of all kinds ever since his mother had run off with the circus or the tinkers. I forget which. Warm greetings were exchanged all around and I handed out bourbons, which is what we drank in the winter. Everyone gathered at my big round kitchen table to be near the ice and await the appearance of the roast. I had comfy chairs and lots and lots of red do-dads in my kitchen so it was hard to keep folks out of there. In no time, we were all aglow from the bourbon and that really hot oven.

"We had a r-r-really interrrresting time, last night," the Irish offered in his Irish whiskey burr-voice.

"Oh, yeah," I mumbled as I glared at that ex-husband, since they'd had that nephew out with them.

"*Yeah*," the nephew chimed in excitedly. "I got to play piano with Jimmy Buffet. He came in the club last night and we all went out later. We stopped by the bar at the Pontchartrain Hotel and they let us noodle around on the piano. It was great!" This was exciting stuff for that nephew, and for us all, really. We'd always been Parrotheads. Partly because Fingers Taylor, Buffet's best harp player is from Mississippi, like me, and an old friend. Of course, Buffet's from Hattiesburg originally. That Mississippi deal is always there.

A week or so later, the story of Nephew/Buffet piano duet was written up in the *Times-Picayune* newspaper. And neither me nor that ex-husband was responsible for it being in the paper. A lot of folks saw it and it was big fun.

I provided another round of bourbons and the three guys began to feel peckish just as the roast had ripened. They were clamoring for shares in the brown dog's roast and snatching the slices as quickly as they slid from my knife. The brown dog's eyes were darting back and forth nervously from the roast to their mouths. He had yet to receive the first taste. What started as a whine of entreaty became snarls of indignation. That dog knew what was fair and this was not it. He maneuvered himself between them and the roast and would not give way. They knew they'd been bested and were obliged to settle for some impromptu nabs. Historically speaking, nabs were little packs of crackers put out by Nabisco and sold in little grocery stores and service stations throughout the rural south. But if it's me talking, then nabs are anything eaten between meals. In this case it happened to be some honey-baked ham, ready-made from a ham store. I had, by the way, invested more time in acquiring that ham than I spend with some members of my family. During the holidays, those ham stores are like a box full of monkeys. They have to have some ham cops on duty to keep people from maiming each other trying to get to the head of the line, which snakes around through those brass poles and velvet ropes. Like at the bank, for crying out loud. "I'd like to withdraw a 5 to 7 pound spiral-sliced ham, please ma'm."

I served the brown dog a very large helping of Christmas roast, with the spicy crust cut off. The guys eagerly snarfed the brown dog's leavings. I took my place at the table to enjoy the Ezra-Brooks-fifteen-year-old. This was some of the best sipping whiskey there ever was, but don't go looking for it. They quit making it. Come December, I remember it fondly as I do the look on that little hound face every year when the brown dog would first lay eyes on his Christmas roast.

Reinventing Divorce

I MEAN TO TELL YOU, during the last few months that me and that ex-husband were living under the same roof, things were pretty ugly.

However, I am proud to report that neither of us allowed anger or loathing or anything to interfere with a therapeutic bit of lolling and fubbing. Let me say a word here to those of us who might undertake an intimate association with a person of the married persuasion: if they tell you they're not sleeping with their spouse, they're probably lying. And to all you wives: if, by some remote chance your husband really isn't sleeping with you, I GUARANTEE YOU HE'S DOING IT SOMEWHERE. What I'm telling you is: guys, especially husbands, are sleeping everywhere they can. And we girls are playing a pretty good game of catch-up, ourownselves.

Me and that ex-husband had some brutal verbal battles. I don't mind saying that I was the meaner of the two of us. I do not "fight fair" because I think it's stupid. That's why they call it a fight instead of a tea-dance.

That husband's favorite gambit—not to be confused with our favorite weekly newspaper, *Gambit*—was playing the nephew card: if you leave, you'll never see that nephew again.

Whereupon I would rejoin, "So what? He's your nephew anyhow and you can just have all the nephew you want"—knowing full well that husband had no desire to actually take over the full time care and feeding of any pubescent other than hisownself.

In spite of the thrill of word-jousting, I was not having nearly as much fun as I was accustomed to. I cheered myself up by wishing him dead and/or thinking up novel ways to kill him. Me and my sister, Jill, wiled away many a cocktail hour going over these plans. We were most inspired upon hearing about this old boy who'd dealt with his wife in a particularly imaginative way. As he told it: "Well, she came climbing through our bedroom window and I mistook her for a raccoon and blasted her with my shotgun." This sounded so much more creative than "I-thought-I-was-shooting-a-burglar." That has just been done to death. I hadn't seen any raccoons in our neighborhood. I think we might have nutria. River rats, for sure.

We pictured me looking fetching-yet-respectable-all-in-black, weeping tastefully without turning my nose red. I yearned for widowhood. I tasted it. I ached for it. I prayed for it. What I absolutely, positively, did not want was to be a grass widow. This is what folks in the south used to call a divorcee. And they'd always said it in the meanest, snidest tone.

I'm not sure where the term grass widow started. It might've come from, "Well, who's going to cut the grass around here, now?" Or it might come from how, in much of the south, when you dig a grave, the red earth is like a fresh, open wound upon the green landscape of the graveyards. When there's divorce, grave digging is hardly ever required so the grass is left intact. Hence, Grass Widow. Catchy though this appellation may be, I did not want it for myself. Also, like a lot of people, I didn't want to have to actually do anything about my life. I wanted better stuff to just happen—and to my specifications.

I couldn't seem to do much, but I could take a break. So me and my sister went on down to Cozumel, near the Yucatan Peninsula of Mexico. I had brought my hostilities with me, so after beaching all day, we'd spend half the night at Guido's plying ourselves with tequila and murderous notions. Before you could say "Pronto," our bellowing alter egos would emerge. One night "Conchita and Consuela" were having a big, loud time—snorting and speaking in tongues. That would be gibberish with our version of a Spanish accent. We are both linguistically challenged. Like when we wanted some hash browns for breakfast and were feverishly pantomiming our desires. Our waiter allowed this to go on for some time before leaning in real close, beaming, to query, "*Fried poh-tay-toes???*"

Yes, I know we sound alluring. Which is why every now and then a lonesome bystander would try to insinuate himself into our deal. Once they'd picked up on the homicidal drift, they would nervously andelay on down the road.

But one was just impervious. So we started in on our expanded hit list. This is where we would name off all the people that we felt were not contibuting much to our sense of well-being or amusement. No matter if they were already dead. The list was extensive and included people who are famous for being innocuous, silly, sanctimonious, smarmy, or smug. Particularly smug. You've got your Roger Staubach, your Mary Lou Retton, your Art Linkletter...

> Barry Manilow
> Tipper Gore
> Pat Sajack *and* Vanna White
> Wink Martindale
> Susan Sarandon
> Bryant Gumbel (but not the brother)
> Judge Judy (but not Dr. Laura—although they
>   might be the same person)
> Anybody who marries a resident of death row
> Barney
> John Warner
> All those Baldwins
> Just about all those TV chefs (except Emeril—we
>   love Emeril)
> That "Painter of Light" (we prefer to do our own

paint-by-numbers, thank you very much)

Pamela Lee

Tommy Lee (but certainly not Tommy Lee Jones)

Kathie Lee Gifford and that Frank

Elliott Gould

Robert Goulet (this one's for you, Elvis!—he couldn't stand Robert Goulet)

Eddie Fisher

Diva facsimiles (for comparison purposes, some real divas worthy of adoration would be Tina Turner, Oprah Winfrey, and my very own DivaSeester, *The* Sweet Potato Queen herownself, Jill Conner Browne).

Never could stand that bandleader that used to be on "Saturday Night Live" that had that piece of hair that swung down in his eye. (I was *stunned* when I learned that my beloved Gilda Radner was once married to that critter.)

So, our interloper butted in with, "Oh, yeah and John Wayne Gacy." And right then was when we invented the sayin': YOU JUST DON'T GET IT, DO YOU? Whereupon the guy whimpers, "Hitler? Or how about Joe McCarthy? Nixon?" We didn't tell him he could've made a couple points with Pat Nixon.

I've given you some of my list. If you don't like those—make your own.

All the chortling and ho-ho-hoing were very good for us. And the folks at Guido's just loved us. We loved them too. Even Guido who is Swiss and can be crabby. The Swiss are not as well known around the world for their crabbiness as they are their clocks and neutrality and bank accounts. But their fellow Europeans know all about it. We had gotten to know Guido and the people at Carlos and Charleys and at the Vista del Mar Hotel over the course of numerous visits. That ex-husband's many visits actually started it all. And me and my seester seemed so very charming by comparison. A lot of people go there to scuba dive which is nice for them. We did not have time because of having to rest and lounge and loll and nap. We did consider strapping knives to our calves like the macho housewives who showed up for "Texas Dive Week." Some people go for the ruins. We are not interested in things that are already ruined.

We were no where near bored, but it was looking pretty much like that husband was not going to up and die. Nor was it likely that I would up and dispose of him. He was going to stay annoyingly alive. Therefore, it was time I headed home to take action. I did the conventional thing and left the son of a bitch. I had made like I was going to leave him a few years earlier—I forget exactly what pissed me off. There were often several choices. I phoned up our good friend, Don Fountain (no relation to Pete). His entire preparation for the Louisiana Bar Exam had taken place in our tavern, so I trusted him.

"Don," I said, "I've got trouble." I am sure he was real surprised to hear that.

"How's that?"

"Tell me what it takes to get an immediate divorce in Louisiana?"

Silence. "Uh, I don't think I ought to be the one advising you..." Don offered.

I replied, "Don, I don't want any advice from you. But you've got all those books sitting right there. Just quote me the law so I don't have to go to the liberry and look this stuff up myself."

"That I can do," he agreed. "Just don't go telling that crazy husband of yours that I so much as read aloud to you."

"I absolutely will not."

"One thing that can get you an immediate divorce is adultery. But you really have to have the goods. It's easy to allege, but pretty hard to prove," Don said.

"Of course, that would be the most obvious way for me to go. I know this school teacher turned private eye, adultery-proving being his specialty. He spies on people between Venetian blinds, key holes, anything. He uses a proctoscope! He could get me some goods. And some laughs, meanwhile."

"Right, I forgot about that guy," Don chuckled.

"But I'm not opening that can of dirt."

"Well, another reason is physical cruelty or abuse," he coninued.

"Those won't do."

"And then, there's habitual intemperance," he offered.

"BINGO!" we said in unison.

Don went on with the wherefores and I swore a great oath not to get Don in trouble. Of course, that very evening, I lambasted that husband with authentic and authoritative sounding legaleez, "I am going to leave your sorry ass and divorce you on the grounds of habitual intemperance. You will be paying alimony for the rest of your life. I am going to ipse your dixit, bucko!" I was gratified that he was momentarily stymied and rueful, both. Excellent combo.

That night, he held forth as usual from behind the bar at the University Inn. Among those on the other side were my quasi-lawyer Don Fountain and Charles Nelson, also an attorney.

"My old lady's been talking to some damned mouthpiece!" that husband bellowed as he reached beneath the bar for the baseball bat. He began to punctuate his remarks with slams of the bat upon the bar. "If I find out," *KA-BLAM!* "Who that son-of-a-bitch is, I'm going to beat the crap out of him with this bat!" *KA-BLAM!*

Fountain froze while Nelson looked on with interest, secure in the knowledge that *he* was not the "mouthpiece." Nelson wondered idly who was such a big fat idiot to get in the middle of this deal—perhaps it was someone new in town.

The slamming of the bat continued, "She said she's going to leave me." *KA-RACK!* "She's going to divorce me for being habitually intemperate," he said mournfully. "It's my damn *job* to be habitually intemperate!" he hollered.

BLAMMO!

I never ratted out Fountain and I didn't leave right then. It took me a whole year longer to get quite enough.

I loved it on moving day when he kept shakin' his head and mumblin', "I just can't *believe* that you are really going to do this. I *love* you. I have *always* loved you."

I almost couldn't believe it myself—that I was really finally gonna leave. Until I did it, I really didn't know for sure if I ever would do it. I was so scared that I would be so scared. But I wasn't! I just did it and I took that nephew with me and not *one word* was said about that. Except by that nephew, who said, "Hot Damn! We should have done this a long time ago."

I did believe him when he said he loved me. Too bad.

I never looked back. You might remember the Bible story, "Lot's Wife." Remember how God told Lot and them to just up and bolt from Sodom and Gomorrah and not to look back? And Lot's wife didn't listen and looked back anyway and God turned her into a pillar of salt.

I was more like the lesser known "Lot's Ex-wife." Umm, hmmm... She was his first wife, having come along several years prior to the story everyone knows so well. (Although wife #2—that salt pillar woman—didn't even get a name. And only one sentence. Pretty short shrift, you ask me.) One day wife #1 woke up and just knew that the time had come to get away from that ole Lot guy and all his trashy friends there in Sodom. He was liable to hang out in Gomorrah sometimes, too. So she packed up all their olive oil jars and bolts of cloth and all the sandals except the ones Lot was wearing at the time and their goats and just most everything and took off. *She did not look back.* She just looked at today and how nice it was without those awful Sodomites and she looked some toward tomorrow, all bright and shiny in the distance and was glad. I think God liked it too, because he did not turn her into anything but just the sweetest thing. Why, everybody that knew her called her "Sugar." So, when some southerner calls you "Sugar," know that it's an homage to that very first "Sugar," way back then. Except for Matt Gregory's knob-globbing Sugar. That was acually her real name—on her birth certificate and everything.

As soon as I got away, I immediately thought of and re-ferred to myself as the ex-wife, and he was of course *that ex-husband* or just X if I got in a hurry. (And to think Lot's ex didn't even get a letter.) And although my mood was some bet-ter, hardly anybody called me "Sugar."

We weren't bona fide ex's because we lived in Louisiana and were both real lazy and afraid of anything involving paperwork and forms to fill out. So it would be years before all of the di-vorce deed would actually be done.

I had no job and no prospects for one. This was mostly be-cause my jobhunting had been done from the convenient van-tage point of my front porch. I could not see any jobs from there. This called for an immediate shifting of gears in the wish-ing-him-dead department. A dead husband was of no use to me now. What I needed was a real reliable, alimony-paying, nephew-support-paying, car-repairing, Nike-buying, alive-and-kicking kind of ex-husband. Moreover, I needed him friendly. I did not need a pissed off ex-husband careening around town with a hard-on for my ass. Not with him knowing way too much about yours truly. Plus his almost total shamelessness left me decidedly outgunned. My friends thought I was being way too paranoid. Wrong buckwheat. They had not had the advantage of being in the tavern and niteclub business. I had seen plenty of bitter ex-husbands in action, all toasted and vocal. Some of my friends would have been mighty attentive to hear exactly which ex-husbands I had seen perform.

Let me give you an example. It's one thing to speak frankly about how you're thinking about breast augmentation since we're all so open and sophisticated and all. Yeah, well. But how about your ex-husband screaming to a barroom full of people, "My ex-old-lady ain't got a tit to her name and she has to wax her upper lip and her behind every Saturday night!" The mere suggestion that I might ever be the subject of one of these impromptu critiques made my blood run cold. I can't even stand the term "old lady." I personally had never augmented or waxed anything, including a floor.

I made up my mind that I was going to do this divorce my way. As a temporary holding pattern while I thought up a plan, I started acting real sweet to that X. I would not be engaging in a knee-jerk, one-sided vendetta because, so far, his position could be classified as neutral—like Switzerland. Nothing is more pitiful than somebody going around dog-cussing a guy who's not paying them any mind at all.

I also started going out of my way to say real nice things about that X behind his back to folks who would be sure to blab. It wasn't long before these things got back to him. Not to be outdone, he started saying nice stuff about me. Not that he'd ever said bad stuff, he just kept his mouth shut. Which will do just fine in a pinch.

Pretty soon, our friends and acquaintances started inviting both of us to the same parties, without a second thought. This was a good sign because there for a while even Bradley over at Clancy's Restaurant had been skittish about having us both up in there at the same time. He probably wouldn't have seriously cared if there'd been a tacky display. New Orleanians love a tacky display. It was never totally out of the question. *I won't wear white shoes before Easter, but I will make a scene with you.*

The divorce deal was easing along fine. I just had the feeling that there was more I could be doing to enhance my position. It was my goal to retain as many of the wifely benefits as possible, even though I was shedding the husband. I left the door to my mind open, like I like to do, to see what would wander in. One evening I was relaxing at that ex-husband's tavern, having been warmly greeted by him and the brown dog. I was seated at the bar availing myself yet again of the cornerstone of my property settlement, the lifetime bar tab. A woman sat down beside me and struck up a chat. "So what's the story on the guy with the brown dog? He's pretty cute," she ventured.

Even though I was still a novice ex-wife, my first thought was to say, "Yeah, that really is a pretty cute dog." I'll admit that my second impulse was to tell her, "Keep your hands off that man, he's mine!" What a notion.

I laughed and did manage to catch myself. Instead I gleefully allowed as how, "Yesssss, indeedy! He certainly is a doll-baby and I am his ex-wife and I would be proud to provide excellent references on his behalf."

Now doll-baby is not a term I would ordinarily apply—I was just trying to be folksy and girly and jolly her up. A doll-baby is more Brad Pitt. He was a much more rugged type, like Russell Crowe. Including that underlying menace. In the face, I always thought he looked like a cross between the young versions of Arnold Palmer and Stacy Keach—specially when he had a mustache.

The woman was struck dumb, so I nattered on that he was fabulous in bed—stamina ahoy—attentive and willing—and a world-class kisser, which, by the way, he was. All of the above. I do know a thing or two about kissing, if I do say so myself and I am not the only one who says so.

She was plainly pleased to have this info, but would have a whole lot rather come by it some other way. The confusion fairly danced across her homely face. (It was an unfortunate coincidence that she was something of a dogball. She had those really long gums and those really short teeth—nubs!)

Anyhow, I was not a bit confused. Clearly, I had found nearly the perfect divorce smoother-over. That ex-husband would shortly know what I had said about him, since I had just provided this ugly woman with a dandy ice-breaker. As soon as I hit the door, she'd be prancing right over to him, simpering and trilling, "Oh do you know that I have just had the most interesting conversation with your ex-wife?" For attention grabbers, I figure that's right up there with, "Hey, blowjobs for everyone!"

When I ran into that ex-husband the very next week, I could tell that my-every-gratifying-word had found its mark. That day and forever after, whenever we would meet or take leave he would deliver me a major smooch. We wouldn't want to lose that world class ranking, now would we?

In case you're thinking all this effort is a big old waste of my time, let me mention a couple of things: A) In New Orleans, you could have somebody killed for $300, and B) Everybody who ever met that ex-husband was scared of him, except for me. I knew that he personally would never hurt me, but it had crossed my mind that he might would hire it done.

Furthermore, there would come the day when he found out what I'd *been* knowing: he'd been *overpaying* my alimony every month for the last four years. Because I had accidentally quoted him an incorrect figure which he then neglected to verify. He did not make me give it back—which he could have done. Nor did he deduct it from future payments, which he also could have done. He just reared back, thumbs in beltloops, and said expansively, "Just consider it a bonus." Which I did.

Even-further-more, as to the suggestion that I might be wasting my time, I always say, "What's time to a pig?" You see, one time there was this farmer who was holding his pig up high so it could reach the apples still on the tree. An outlander wandered by and said, "Hey! Isn't that a waste of time?" The farmer countered with: "What's time to a pig?"

Still-further-more, there was the day I dropped by the old tavern after a particularly trying day and wondered out-loud—"What are the chances of my getting laid?"

"Real good," that ex-husband responded, even out louder.

I stood up expectantly.

"Oh, you mean now?" he queried.

"Whaddya think? That I want to make an appointment for next Thursday? Of course, *now*," I snapped.

He hopped up and led the way upstairs. I made note of the fact that he'd only asked "when" and not "by whom."

At the top of the stairs there was an awkward silence that broke apart in giggles and snorts. We were nothing if not cosmopolitan. "It's not like we've never done this before," we gasped. But, in fact, that's just what it was like. The First Time. The years rolled back and we were where we started before all that nasty water ran under our bridge. Back where we used to sit across from each other, blabbing away. Eyes would lock and if somebody didn't look away, we'd shortly be flushed and panting and running off to go at it like dogs in the first available place. Or like missionaries or whooping cranes. It was like that again in his moldy, upstairs "office." From downstairs came the sounds of the best jukebox in New Orleans. It was playing his favorite oldie—"Who's Makin' Love to Your Ole Lady While You Were Out Makin' Love?" A question that had oft been pondered by his own guilty heart.

We finished our feverish private dance, as pleased as we could be with ourselves. Then we went back down the stairs to enjoy another beverage and listen to my favorite oldie, "Mr. Pitiful." Present company excepted—I just like the song.

I would say that here was as polite and accommodating an ex-husband as a body could want. Amen to civility and pass that Tish Baldridge Award!

This started me thinking. Compliments and kindness and cajolery seemed to work so well on that ex-husband. I wondered if our marriage mightn't have gone a bit better if I'd have been a little less hateful. I wondered if there were communication skills that were more effective than seething and snarling and frothing and relentless browbeating. Like many divorced people, I wondered "What if this" and "What if that" and "What if I had done things differently?"

What I think is that most folks really don't want to do anything at all ever. But they do wish, sometimes fervently, that things had turned out better. Well, lemme tell you something: If you really do wish you had it to do over, well, you do. Starting today. Any day. In any way. Get up in the morning and do it over. Different. If you keep doing stuff the same way over and over, expecting a different outcome, that is beyond stupidity. It is, in fact, lunacy. Anyway, don't do that.

Here's the little plan I started out with. I am going to:

1. START EACH DAY FRESH. No being mad over leftovers. I will find new and exciting things to get mad at.

2. TREAT THAT EX-HUSBAND AS I WOULD A STRANGER. One who has not yet done anything to piss me off. (Stuff that did not work on a husband sure as hell won't work with an ex-husband.)

3. CONSIDER THE NOTION THAT THE CAREFULLY DETAILED, CARVED IN STONE IMAGE I'VE BEEN CARRYING AROUND IN MY HEAD—right above the title "Happiness"—MIGHT COULD STAND A RETOUCH. Or I could even discard it altogether and start with an empty canvas called "No Expectations." How could a half-way clever person have spent even one day thinking that in this full and fancy world there is only one way to be happy? Maybe you can't have *that* thing, but you can still have a *good* thing!

4. TRY TO REMEMBER THAT IT IS STUPID TO EXPECT LOGIC FROM LUNATICS. They are dang near impossible to manage, predict, or understand. So sitting around trying to figure them out is a major waste of time.

5. TRY TO REMEMBER THAT GUYS ARE NOT REALLY HAIRY GIRLS IN BOY CLOTHES. They are not like us at all. I mentioned this to that nephew who snorted and said, "Yeah, I know, we're more like dogs in pants."

The Practice Brown Dog

RASCAL WAS HIS NAME. He was a brown dog. He began as our part time dog. His official owner was E.B. who was our downhill neighbor when I was growing up in Jackson, Mississippi. But as soon as Rascal got to know us, he liked us a lot better than E.B. and them. He started out making short visits, chiefly at mealtimes. It could have been due to the leftovers that were on our front porch. We figured that Rascal was not getting enough to eat at home since he was digging in our garbage. To test the theory, we put some food outside and, proof positive, he was right there each time. Then one dinnertime, we didn't put anything out there. We had either forgotten or else we wanted it all for ourselves. Anyway, we were pretty well tucked into mother's fried chicken when we heard somebody knocking at the front door. It turned out to be Rascal banging against the screen door. He was way too short to reach the doorbell.

We invited him in and he accepted with alacrity. Mother fixed him a plate in the kitchen and that was all she wrote. We had us a full time dog and nobody had to tell us how to treat one, either. We were all born knowing that a dog will tell you what he wants; all you need do is listen and watch. For instance, it didn't take my mother any time at all to figure out that Rascal preferred his chicken gizzards fried crispy—and livers too. If he could get them. Mother was partial to the livers herownself. And if there was going to be dog food, then it must be Mitey Dog. He didn't care for any other canned dog food and wouldn't even look at the dry kind. I guess his favorite food was the same as ours—mother's fried chicken. I've tried to talk her into cooking and selling her chicken at the New Orleans Jazz and Heritage Festival. They've got a group that sells some pretty fine chicken out there, but my mama's is even better. And it's not just cause she's my mama—some of her stuff is not that great. But she's got that chicken down. The main ingredient she puts into it is TIME. She takes a real long time to fix it and it cannot be done any other way. I know because I have tried many times to trick the chicken into thinking it's done. The chicken comes out looking just perfect, but it's bloody by the bone. I'm going to tell you the right way to do chicken and sometime when you've got a couple of hours to spare, well, you try it.

Judy's Mama's Fried Chicken

*1 fryer plus many extra wings because it's Judy and her
    sister's favorite chicken part*
All purpose flour
salt
*black pepper, cayenne pepper and paprika (if you don't
    like spicy, don't put much)*
good, light vegetable oil like canola
milk or buttermilk
big, heavy skillet and cover
*platter and bowl—both big enough to hold all chicken
    parts*
paper sack and brown paper or paper towels or newspaper

At least two hours before you want to eat you must be in possession of some fresh or thawed out chicken. Rinse it real good
in cold running water. Pat dry. Salt and let sit for about 10 or 15
minutes. Then put all parts in bowl and cover with milk or buttermilk (cold water with salt in it is better than nothing—in
case you're like me and won't go to the store for just one thing
unless it's made out of chocolate or is toilet paper). Put chicken
in the refrigerator for an hour.

In that paper sack, mix together the flour, both peppers and
paprika. I use a lot, more than mother even. Put about $1/_4$ inch-
worth of oil in the skillet and turn fire to medium. Put 3 pieces
of chicken at a time in the sack and shake til covered well with
flour mixture.

When oil is hot, start adding chicken parts. The object is to
brown chicken slowly first on one side, then the other, then
first side again. Try to have something soothing to think about
or listen to so you won't get in a hurry. Not being real hungry
would help.

Drain on brown paper if possible. It is best served at a bit
above room temperature, so mind you don't food poison everybody. Let cool about 15 minutes, then either eat it or refriger-

ate it. There won't be any leftover. If you need some left over,
you will have to get you a hiding place. (Like you don't already
have one.)

Rascal was crazy about the Mitey Dog television commercials because he felt they spoke to issues of interest to him. Those items would be that he was on the small side and he had decidedly short legs—so short that they didn't exactly match the body he'd been given. All the Mitey Dogs had short legs.

Rascal thought of himself as a mighty dog. We did too. In fact, we'd often greet him with a hearty, "It's Mighty Dog!!" He liked that a lot.

More and more of Rascal's time was spent at our house. E.B. didn't even miss him at night because he thought Rascal was sleeping outside like always. I have never understood why anybody would want a pet to keep outside. Unless it's a pony. I know for a fact that anybody who keeps a dog outside on a chain is going straight to hell. If you want to have a real, working guard dog, then get the thing trained so you don't need to chain it up. Besides, here's a bulletin for idiots: There is the odd criminal who is capable of measuring the length of a chain. Back to the going to hell deal: anyone who mistreats an animal in any way, if you so much as hurt their feelings, you are going straight to hell.

I guess we were engaging in a form of dognapping. Definitely alienation of affections. We told ourselves, and I think we were right, that Rascal had hardly any affection for E.B. anyhow. Therefore, so what? We went head on. We hit a home run the night E.B. came home late and kinda loaded. It was about three in the morning; this was plenty late enough for Jackson, Mississippi. Seemed like he'd been having some beer somewhere. Quite a bit of beer. He pulled into his driveway, but didn't pull into his garage. Probably because he was afraid he might hit something. He turned off everything, and made to get out of his car. That first foot wasn't on the pavement good when something had a hold of his ankle. Rascal had rushed from the backyard and caught hisself a late nighter. Rascal had a grip and would not let go. E.B. was hollering at him to let go and trying to beat him about the head. But Rascal was quick and, like we said, mighty, and he bit the hell out of E.B.'s leg. My father was quick to seize the advantage in the war for the affections of Rascal. E.B. was already at some disadvantage here, being unaware that there was a battle. He just thought he was mighty lucky to have a dog who was hardly ever hungry and never whined to come inside his house. Anyway, Daddy threw open a window on the downhill side of the house and bellowed into the night, "HEY! E.B.! IF YOU GOT HOME AT A DECENT HOUR, MAYBE YOUR OWN DOG WOULD KNOW YOU!"

After that Rascal just out and out lived with us and E.B. gave up all pretense that Rascal was his dog. Or ever had been, for that matter. I think it's kind of funny how that went, on account of how now you read about neighbors hitting each other in the head with shovels over the least thing. If my Daddy were alive today, he'd have to live way out in the country. He used to do stuff like spank other peoples' kids! I can't hardly believe it.

People don't even spank their own children anymore. Come to think of it, our Daddy didn't spank us either. All the kids always wanted to play at our house because we really did have the best daddy. So fun. They surely weren't flocking to play with us—because we were very bossy. One time this kid even rang the bell and asked could Judy's Daddy come out and play!! I just said that he could not because he was at work. I hadn't learned to say stuff like, "Why don't you just go on home and play with your own raggedy-ass Daddy!"

However, kids were not allowed to tear up stuff or each other while they were at our house. A couple of them didn't get it. These two six-year-olds set about making themselves at home. Daddy told them, "Ya'll can't play in the sand box today because somebody left the cover off last night and the cats have used it for their bathroom." And then he went back to enjoying his wood chopping. When he took a breather and looked around the yard, he spotted the two boys just as they shat in the sandbox.

So he spanked them. They were stunned! They whined that they were going to tell their daddies. He said, "Good, tell them to come on down here; they probly need spanking too." Nobody went and got their daddy that day. Or any other day.

Nothing more would ever be said about their misbehaving and those kids were only too glad to be welcomed back.

I guess what may have saved the Rascal situation from getting unfriendly was that Rascal was not, after all, a treasure. (Perhaps it was the same in the case of the spanked kids.) He was not a fabulous dog. He was a very crabby dog. He once bit one of my mother's friends totally without preamble. She was a real mild-mannered lady, just standing in the yard chatting with mother. Rascal just marched right up to her and bit the crap out her calf, which he could barely reach. We fussed at him but he was not a bit sorry. Luckily for Rascal, the lady was too mild-mannered to extract her pound, or whatever amount, of flesh from him, which she was certainly entitled to do. Furthermore, she didn't try to extract money from us. Would this happen nowadays? I don't think so. My family has more than used up it's nine lives in the litigation department.

So, Rascal was a starter dog. He was my introduction into the world of brown dogs, which is vast. They all look so much alike but they have got the best and most varied personalities. I am really not interested in spending time with any other kind. Although, I think it is just fine if you want to. If so, I urge you to consider the Schipperke. It's a pure bred Belgian dog that lives fifteen years easy.

The brown dog was nothing like Rascal. Except for the brown part, of course. And the crabby part. The brown dog was crabby sometimes. But Rascal kept a frown on his face and was just your all around curmudgeon, whereas, the brown dog was often smiling and laughing. He was just filled with good cheer, as long as you didn't annoy him. We could even interfere a bit with his eats and he'd be okay with it. Rascal, being a deprived dog, couldn't bear that. He'd been forced to do without by the unenlightened E.B. for too long to ever relax about his food needs or any other needs for that matter. Whereas, the brown dog had gotten plenty of everything right from the start and, so, was able to go through life with a certain confidence in that regard. There was definitely the trust factor. The brown dog would never have entertained the first notion that we would fail to see to his needs. Rascal, on the other hand, was like some people you meet who feel they've been shortchanged all their lives. They act like they've got to scratch and scramble for everything they get. Then they jealously guard their pitiful mess of potage, whatever it might be. Also, I think they spend way too much time worrying about what's on the other fellow's plate.

If Rascal were in the house and you were not either sleeping or fixing him something to eat, then you'd better have been paying him some attention. He desired constant physical contact. Whereas the brown dog was quite content to go off on his own. He was fairly sociable, interacting in a number of ways with other dogs. Rascal was completely antisocial. He wasn't "fixed," but we were pretty sure he was a virgin. His social life consisted of chasing all other dogs out of the yard while trying to bite them in the butt. It worked for him. Like it does for some people.

A Courting We Will Go

T HE BROWN DOG WAS ABOUT A YEAR OLD when it came time for me and that X to officially untie the marital knot. The banana-republican laws we had at the time made the process long and complicated. Lots of Louisianans stayed married, not just because they're Catholics, of which there are tons, but because it was so damn much trouble to call it quits. However there was a bright spot in this dark ages situation: alimony! Louisiana was among the few states that still provided for alimony—under certain circumstances. Namely, the party "at fault" could be made to fork it over to the unfaulted party. I might as well tell you that it was widely known back then that nothing was ever my fault. In fact, hardly a day would go by without me saying, "Not my fault."

This is as good a time as any to pass along a warning: mind how you step down the aisle in Louisiana. We've got this deal now called the "Covenant Marriage" that is serious hog-tying. I don't think you can even rid yourself of an ax-murderer—unless they murder you, of course. Then it's moot. Moot is one of the main tools for conflict resolution around here: you stand around, mouth breathing, until the thing becomes moot. A couple of people I know have been lured into these covenant marriages under the misguided notion that they were signing up for the "Deluxe Wedding." They wanted everything to be first class, don't you know?

I had always been a stand-up woman, liberated, independent, looked out for myself, yada, yada, yada. By the by, I was using yada way before Seinfeld and I might even be able to prove it. I started saying it right when we elected a judge here in town named Yada McGee. I'd never heard that name before and really took to it. Same thing with alimony. From the first time I heard it, I just purely loved the notion and wanted some for myself in the worst way.

That X had enlisted two of our many, many attorney friends to represent us "free gratis," as New Orleanians are fond of saying. We are up to our butts in lawyers here. There are more lawyers than bartenders, even. That makes us very litigious and our insurance rates very high.

One of our lawyers was Paul Mistrano, cracker-jack criminal lawyer and hell of a nice guy. He routinely handled that ex-husband's fairly frequent runnings-afoul-of-the-law. Most of the stuff that X did would have been beneath the dignity of any self-respecting 15-year-old. But nothing was too juvenile or embarrassing for him.

The other draftee was "Sparky," the last of the line of an old and pretty famous local family. Unlike a lot of those families, his had not yet spent up all of the money. So Sparky mostly ran for public office and sat around dreaming up grandiose, unlikely schemes for grabbing power and more money.

The night before we were to have our day-in-court, I phoned up that X. "Can you give me a ride down to the courthouse tomorrow?"

"Yeah," he agreed, "And we oughta go by and get Sparky too—to be sure he makes it there... By the way, Sparky will be representing you."

"I might have known you'd take the good lawyer for yourself," I carped.

It didn't really much matter since we had worked out the details on our own anyway. This was a truly remarkable feat, for which I take all of the credit, since that X behaved like he'd been raised by wild dogs. Just in case something untoward should arise in the courtroom, I had rigged myself out in Rebecca-of-Sunnybrook-Farm-fashion—you know, blonde hair loose and long, demure and dowdy dress, bland expression. (If you whisper the word "Limb" it sets your mouth just right to convey innocence and dignity and stuff like that.)

Even so, he arrived promptly at my door the next morning, looking fetching in one of his many brown outfits. I also deserve full credit for his promptness. I taught him that and to always pay his bills. I heard he got a little lax in both these areas after I left—but not in any way that would affect me.

The ugly brown outfits were his own doing; I hate brown, myself. In anything but dogs. I glanced past him to his big brown convertible and spotted that brown dog—riding shotgun.

"That dog is not going!" I snapped.

Silence.

"That dog is *not* going to court with us. I am not going *through* this shit with you today!"

That ex-husband had recently begun this goofy business of tying to smuggle the brown dog in everywhere he went. There had been a bru-ha-ha or two and they'd been bounced. For instance, the Superdome. Dogs used to go to the ballgames at Tulane University's Sugar Bowl Stadium all the time. Like this black and white dog we knew named Jason. He was quite the sports fan. He went to many games, as he had no difficulty getting inside. And once inside, he knew exactly what to do when security came near and people hollered, *"RUN, JASON, RUN!"* The Superdome, however, is a real tight ass place. They are not even all that welcoming to their human guests. And, it's a tight squeeze, too. You cannot apply mustard without getting it on your neighbor's weenie. These football fans here are the most loyal, long-suffering people in the world.

Man and dog also made an attempt to breach one of the Inaugural Balls for either the mayor or the governor, I forget which. This time, it was really that X who drew the fire before they even had a chance to consider the prospect of the brown dog's admission. The occasion was black tie, so that ex-husband put on what he liked to wear to formal events: yellow pants with yellow and green checkedy shirt. Summer or winter, black tie, white tie, inside, outside—whatever—he wore the yellow ensemble. Possibly because it was his most noticeable outfit.

"I mean it," I said. "We've got to go to court and we don't have time to jack with the dog."

Silence.

Silence.

"Oh alright, the dog can go, but he doesn't get to drive and he'll have to wait in the car for us!" I conceded—if we were ever going to get this show on the road. Another clever thing that X had taken to doing was letting the dog drive his car. The Brown Dog would get in the driver's seat and put his arms on the steering wheel, while that X rode shotgun. With his long legs and semi-simian arms, that X could operate the pedals and the steering from his side of the car, undetected by pedestrians. Down the street they'd go, Brown Dog grinning over the wheel. One time, when that X went to stick his head out the passenger window by way of further role reversal, he let go of the steering wheel and the big, brown convertible careened onto the sidewalk. There were no people in the way, but the Brown Dog scored a couple of trash cans before that X could stop the car. One homeowner ventured curbside to voice a complaint about his mangled property. Meanwhile, that X scooted over, trading places with his driver and explained to the citizen, "Sorry,

buddy, but look, it's not my fault, the dog was the one driving!"
And off they went.

That ex-husband grinned happily and sprang to open the car
door for me to demonstrate goodwill. Years before we'd engaged
in a war of wills over the opening of car doors. One of my few
victories. I guess you can tell that I didn't always put as much
thought into my choice of battles as I might have. This was not
much of a hill to die on. Also, on this day, I beat out the brown
dog for the shotgun seat.

We set off for Sparky's house in the Irish Channel. It's
called that because the Irish, who came here to dig the canals
and die of fever doing it, had settled in that neighborhood.
Some had survived, but their descendents mostly moved
away—to the suburbs. They come back every year for the Saint
Patrick's Day Parade that rolls down Magazine Street, which
used to be Main Street for the Channel. The Irish have been
replaced by other groups of up-and-comers. Right now, it's Af-
rican-Americans and Hispanics and disgruntled suburbanites
moving back to the city. They got sick of the commute and they
don't even know what a real one is.

Sparky's car was in his driveway, but no one would answer
the door. That ex-husband shinnied up the drain thing and
banged on a second floor window. He had performed this stunt
at our home many times when he'd forgotten his key. I really
could have shot him and gotten away with it.

Directly, a bristling topnotch of "morning hair" attached to
the pounding, throbbing, hungover head of lawyer Sparky

popped up above the window sill. He waved that he'd be along. Eventually, preceded several feet by last night's fumes, he presented himself curbside. He had anointed himself liberally with cologne in futile attempt at masking the Jack Daniels. The seersucker suit he had selected had come from the bottom of the pile and it was redolent of garlic and grease from, I would guess, Parasol's, since it was near his house. He probably had a lot of his meals there. When he wasn't conferring at Galatoire's. If you're going to wear something from off your floor, seersucker is a wise choice as it looks wrinkled anyway and the stripes hide the footprints. I bet there haven't been a dozen seersucker suits sold outside of New Orleans in fifty years. It's the summer uniform here. Even for guys with lots better taste.

We made Sparky sit in the back seat with the brown dog. They sized each other up. The brown dog gave Sparky a thorough sniff-over and was not at all approving. The two began jockeying for the middle spot. Sparky won and leaned over the front seat the whole way, breathing and blathering all over me and that ex-husband.

When we got to the courthouse, we found a parking place right in front, thanks to my late father. When he was alive, he was nearly phobic when it came to inconvenience—his own or any of his family's. If he couldn't get a spot in front of it, he wouldn't go to it. Since he died, he has really been bearing down on the parking situation. I don't think I've missed but a couple of appointments or events on account of not finding a place right in front.

Outside the courtroom we found that ex-husband's lawyer, Paulie, all fresh and bright-eyed and three-piece-suited and mustache-combed. He went over the procedure with us. He told that X, "Okay, so you'll be at fault and..."

"Wait, wait," that ex-husband interjected. "It wasn't my fault, *she* left *me*."

"We know that, and I'm sure it was just out of the blue and you hadn't been doing any of your rattin' around," Paulie said crisply.

"Uhmmmmmmmmm..." that ex-huband rejoined.

"Look, you know very well that we do not have 'no fault' divorce here yet," Paulie continued, "It will look real bad for her to be at fault. Only trashy women are at fault. But, somebody's got to be, so you're elected, sport!"

"Okay, okay, I'll be at fault," he agreed, as though agreeing to be "It" in a game of tag.

I was thinking how nice it was that everyone was so concerned about me not appearing to be trashy. I don't mind being trashy, but I sure don't want to appear to be. I also figured that nobody was going to bring up the A-word. And I would have bet a big ole hunk of money on that fact. Nope, none of these three would mention adultery. And if I did I'd be faced with six big round innocent eyes and three mouths open in baffled surprise. The life-long charade would not end today.

"Now, what about the grounds?" Paulie asked. "We could just do abandonment."

"No, we can't," that ex-husband insisted mulishly. "*She* left *me*."

Paulie gave an exasperated sigh, "Oh, good grief. Well, then, how about cruel treatment?"

"You mean, like, I *beat* her?" that ex-husband wondered apprehensively.

"No. No... it would be mental cruelty."

"That's good. Let's do that one!" that ex-husband agreed eagerly.

My lawyer had thus far contributed a series of *uh-huhs* and a couple of *yesindeeds*, while fondly massaging his paunch.

We all filed into the courtroom and sat down together near the rear to wait our turn among the other happy couples and their entourages. Meanwhile, my lawyer had lapsed into dreamy reverie, burping softly to himself while smiling vaguely.

"Paulie..." I began worriedly.

"It's all right. Don't worry, I'll take care of everything," Paulie assured.

Once in a while it is really great to run up on a man who takes charge. It's like when you go dancing: it's really refreshing when you run up on a guy who says, "Hey, can I lead?"

When there was a break in the lawyerly action, Paulie went up to the bench and whispered at some length to the judge, who looked startled and then stared curiously at us.

Paulie called that ex-husband to the stand and asked him a few questions. Then he said to the judge, "If it please the court, I'll also be representing the wife in this case. She *is* represented by counsel, who *is* present in this courtroom. However, your honor, her counsel is at present... indisposed."

Sparky nodded at the judge and smiled proudly.

The judge was not smiling, but he did nod his acceptance of the deal. Paulie continued questioning that ex-husband, "Did you treat your wife in a cruel manner?"

"OH, YES!" that ex-husband beamed at the judge and then at me like a third-grader who knows the right answer.

"Did you tell her you no longer love her?" Paulie asked.

Silence. Uncertainty filled that ex-husband's face. They had not rehearsed this question, but you could tell that he was pretty sure he'd never said *that.*

I caught his eye and nodded my head vigorously while mouthing silently, "Do *not* f--- this up!"

He mumbled grudgingly, "Well, I might have..." The judge looked bemused, but went on and rendered our community asunder. And: *yip-yip-yahoo-ALIMONY FOR MEEEEE!!!*

Not that this was any big surprise to me because, like I said, we had made the whole agreement between ourselves already. But one always has to get the official stamp on this stuff because you just don't know what will happen on down the line. Like, what if that ex-husband were to take up with some women who had a lot of backbone and a whole bunch of kids who could convince him to quit paying me and give her the money. That's why a handshake just isn't enough.

We exited amid stares. In a fit of pre-nostalgia, I thought to myself, "This is the last time I will ever be stared at because of this son-of-a-bitch."

Guess again, buckwheat. That turned out to be not quite true. But it did mark the end of my giving a rat's ass. It sure took me for-damn-ever to learn not to feel responsible for what other people do.

If you are trying to be the boss of somebody else, especially someone who won't mind worth a damn, I urge you to give it up. You will feel great, I promise.

Once outside the courthouse, my scraggly-ass lawyer perked right up, "Let's go celebrate!" Sparky screamed.

Me and that ex-husband agreed. It was sort of like how when you're at Schoen Funeral Home on Canal Street for a wake, you just have to go across the street to Mandina's afterward for some drinks and some marinated crab claws. This is closure in New Orleans. It can also bring new beginnings; a lot of new partnerships have started at the "apres funeral."

Of course, the brown dog was always ready to extend any outing. But Paulie very responsibly went on back to his office, since it was only 11:00 in the AM, and, unlike some lawyers, he actually had some real clients.

"Let's go to Bacatown to this place I know," Sparky offered.

Bacatown refers to the area on the side of Esplanade Avenue that is not the French Quarter—originally "Back of town." It was not yet enjoying the gentrification that had swept through some other neighborhoods. We pulled up to a rundown little corner grocery, parked the big brown convertible and got out. The brown dog had a pit stop at the leafless stick that was the lone tree on that block. From the outside, the place did not appear to be open for business. But it was. I'm not sure that the wheels of commerce turned much, judging by the sparsely stocked shelves. If you were in the market for local favorites like Bengal Roach Spray, or Tabasco Sauce, or Zatarain's Crab Boil, you were in good shape. You would also be set if you were hunting twenty-five-year-old jars of olives or anchovy paste, whose labels were nearly obscured by rust and dust. But the biggest movers were the half pints of booze which customers took away in little brown bags for nipping as they sauntered about the neighborhood or sat chatting on their front stoops.

We got the nod from the pasty-faced cashier, us and the brown dog too. Sparky led the way through a door behind the counter. The door and its frame were black and coated thick with several decades-worth of undisturbed filth. I managed not to make contact; the guys took no notice; the brown dog was pretty intrigued by such a potpourri of evidence to investigate.

The backroom was full of smoke and empty beer cases and an extremely animated assortment of citizens. They were perched on nail kegs and an old church pew, huddled around a rickety table, conferring loudly over poker dice. The dice were almost as nasty as the doorway. Originally ivory with black sunken dots, they were so stained with nicotine that it was hard to make out the dots. And the corners had their sharpness buffed away by a jillion tumbles across the table.

The guys were greeted cheerily with "Hey ho's" and back-slaps, while I received head bob's and "Howdee do's." And the brown dog forestalled the formalities by baring his teeth and with a growl, repaired to a corner for a little nap. He had had a busy morning, guarding the convertible and all the emotion of the divorce and putting up with Sparky and all.

The guys made room at the table for us and our fresh money. My grub-stake was provided by that ex-husband. I thought his equanimity in this matter boded well for our future financial encounters.

Sparky was very lively and very much in charge, since he was no stranger to this establishment. Unlike the courthouse, where his face had been no more recognized than mine.

We consumed a thousand Abita Turbodog beers and shot craps til nearly dark. Everyone suddenly recalled that they had stuff to do and bustled importantly off into the twilight.

Our group piled back into the big, brown convertible for the ride back Uptown. This trip, the brown dog absolutely refused to get in the back seat with Sparky. So, he sat up front between me and that ex-husband. Every now and then he'd look back over his shoulder at Sparky and curl his lip in a self-satisfied sneer over his superior placement.

Sparky wanted to be dropped at his other office—the Half Moon Bar in the Irish Channel. After that we cruised on to my house, enjoying the evening air with its familiar grain elevator smell from across the river and wondering what Paulie had whispered to that judge. Perhaps, something like, "Please bear with me, your honor. These people are squirrels. Let's just be done with them and move them on out of here."

I bid a fond adieu to the brown dog and that ex-husband walked me to my front door. "Uh, I'm sorry about that stuff I said down at the court. I didn't mean it," he mumbled. He bid me an even fonder good evening with an enthusiastic kiss. "I still love you," he asserted with equal vigor.

"I know," I answered, while thinking to myself, *and you will for the rest of your miserable life, buddy.* "That's okay," I said. "I still love you, too."

I waved goodbye as they drove out of sight. They were honking and barking and laying rubber—not an easy thing to do in a car the size of a yellow school bus.

It had not been a bad day at all—once again proving my theory that you can have a good time almost anywhere. Plus, I had won fifty bucks and remembered to scrub the poker dice crud off my hands before touching my face or anything in my home.

Making Your Own Fun

ONE TIME ME AND THAT EX-HUSBAND got invited to a party. We were always getting invited to parties. On the way to this one, we ran into this guy, Dix. Everybody just called him that because he drove a Dixie Beer truck. This caused him to be in that ex-husband's tavern at least once a week on a delivery. Usually, he'd be there more than that as a sometime player in the University Inn Follies. These were the often elaborate games and scenarios that would be played out up in there, under the direction of that ex-husband. He didn't plan this stuff out. It was pretty much pure improvisation. And a lot of it was priceless.

Dix was wearing his usual beer truck driving outfit. It looked like a bowling get-up with "Dixie" emblazoned over the shirt pocket. He had ditched the hat because his hair was a source of great pride. The thick, wavy, naturally-black-as-coal locks were well-coated with gel to maintain the pompadour. And not a hair moved, from early morning, through a whole day of slinging cases of beer, in all kinds of weather. Dix was unfailingly well-coifed. He was cheerful and secure in the solid belief in his own personal attractiveness and innate brilliance. I would not say that this belief was universally shared. I'm not saying Dix was a troll. Not at all. In fact, you could have buffed him up and taken him most anywhere. Could have. Theoretically. But smart money said stay near the door. Always a good idea.

With Dix in his customary fine fettle, that ex-husband urged him to come on and go with us to this party. He figured Dix would be a breath of fresh air to the Tulane University students and some faculty who'd be at this deal. Dix thought so too. Off we went.

Upon entering the smallish upstairs apartment, we found ourselves standing among a bunch of people arrayed on the living room floor. They were the usual tweedy sorts found at Tulane parties. Some actually wore those jackets with the patches on the elbows. And the lapels were always from another decade. Nobody ever wore anything that looked new. And female legs were usually hairy. They were all sitting or squatting pretty close together around these two guys who had the only two chairs in the room. It was obvious that the pair was the main attraction. Not just because they got the good seats; everyone was turned toward them and I could hear the breath baiting. This is different, I thought.

That X and Dix didn't seem to notice anything except that the bar was not in this room. They picked their way among the gathering and I followed them through the swinging door to the kitchen. We found the bar and a few folks standing around chatting. Among them was Hiram the Scot, a math professor known for his thrift and his singing voice. And for a limited repertoire. He contributed just the one song. A very fine one called "The Highland Tinker." When Hiram sang it, it came out "The Heeland Tinker." He came to the University Inn and taught it to all of us and it got sung most every night. It went sort of like this:

Oh, the lady of the manor was preparing for a ball
When she spied the Heeland Tinker, tossing off against the
* wall.*
So the lady wrote a letter and in it she did say,
"I'd rather be f---ed by you, sir, than my husband any day."
Well, he rode up to the manor and he strode up thru the
* hall,*
God save us, cried the butler, for he's come to f--- us all.
He f----ed 'em in the stairwell and he f--ed 'em in the hall,
But when he f---ed the butler, twas the finest f--- of all.
Now the tinker's dead and buried, buried in St. Paul's,
It took four and twenty choir boys just to carry in his balls.

Chorus: With his bloody red kidney wiper
And his bollocks a-hanging free

And a yard-and-a-half of foreskin hanging down
below his knees

We would sing the chorus after each couplet to make it last longer. It was pretty cheery.

I greeted Hiram the Scot and inquired what was the deal with the two dudes in the parlor.

Hiram gleefully imparted, "Oh, those are Allen Ginsberg and Lawrence Ferlinghetti. They are going to do a reading."

I shared this information with that ex-husband and Dix, who wondered, "Reading? Out loud? What the hell are they going to read?"

"I should think it would be poems. They are poets," I suggested. I had heard of them.

"Po —ettts?" Dix whined, "Oh, f---."

"Yes, well," I responded. "Didn't anyone mention this when they invited us?" I asked that ex-husband.

"Hmm. I don't think so," that X said.

I believed him. Aside from "The Heeland Tinker" and some limericks, he'd never shown much interest in verse. I can't claim to be much less of a Philistine my ownself. I like the poetry of Stephen Crane—yeh that "Red Badge of Courage" guy and, of course, Chris Champagne, my good friend and unofficial poet laureate of New Orleans.

I was raised hearing about the wigwam of Nokomis. My father would burst into poetry at the drop of a hat. He went to school in a one-room schoolhouse. With all those grades to teach at once, the teacher made them memorize a whole lot to keep them occupied. And would beat them if they didn't.

Sometimes the teacher would send an offending kid outside to cut the very switch with which he would have the crap beat out of him. And my father tended to offend quite a bit. In fact, his name, John Albert Conner, was legend thereabouts for his creative misdeeds.

One time, Daddy and his good friend wanted to create a diversion. This was before routine fire drills were invented. The pair had come early to school that day and were rooting around in the closet known as the cloak room. Each pupil had a cubby of his own where he could keep personal items, besides his cloak. In one cubby they spied an old flour sack. It belonged to this boy who was notorious for his tennis shoes. This was because he wore them every day, rain or shine, to the cow barn, to the pig pen, and to school. They were positively juicy. They made slurping noises when he walked. And they were in the flour sack. Daddy and his friend took the flour sack and shoved it inside the woodstove that was the heat source for the classroom. The intention was to hide the guy's shoes. But they went outside and forgot about them. Until the teacher called everyone in and they saw that a fire was already going in the stove. And the stench was going good, too. Without even looking inside the stove or asking any questions of anybody, the teacher turned a glittering eye to Daddy and his hapless cohort. Which is where he always looked when there was blame to be laid and ninety per cent of the time he'd be right.

He said, "John Albert, you two go out back and cut me some switches." Each boy would receive a beating with the switch cut by his friend. This was the Ethel, MS version of psychological gamesmanship. Daddy's friend came right back with a piddling little twig. Our Daddy was gone a looooonng time. It took him a good hour to cut down that sapling because all he had was a rusty pocket knife. He dragged the tree into the school house by the trunk. He went all the way to the front of the class, right to the teacher's desk, but the tree top still wasn't inside the door. Checkmate.

Of course, he was out of school more than he was in. He was a farm kid and had to help do the crop thing. And then there were the times he missed because he did not have any shoes to wear. Which was okay during the spring part, but was very embarrassing in the winter. Not to mention cold. And he was out sick a lot, too.

And according to my father, his family was better off than a lot of people. Especially poor city people. Because farm folks always had plenty to eat. Nothing to wear or drive or play with. Except at Christmas, when the old shoe boxes would be filled with a couple of oranges. They could not spare any socks to be hanging by the chimney with care, so they used the old shoe boxes. I bet those younguns were thrilled come Christmas morn. There's nothing quite like whiling away an afternoon playing with your oranges. I think that po' folks with sense don't buy fruit out of season. For what they paid for the damn oranges in

December they could have gotten a nice jack-in-the-box or a bag of marbles.

After my father died, I cleaned out his office. I found a yellow legal pad where he'd started to write down some of his childhood recollections:

It was Christmas Eve, 1926. The old house was quiet, though it was home to four children, John Albert, the youngest child, and his three sisters. Smoke poured from the two chimneys and light from the fires shown out of the windows. Sleet rattled the tall windows and the wind moaned around the corners. Death had hovered over the old house for the last six days as John Albert fought pneumonia, a mostly fatal condition at that time.

"Grannie," taken in by the family when she had nowhere else to go but who was no relation to them, stood watch in the sick room. She had predicted that tonight would be the turning point; it would likely be life or death before dawn for the boy. Grannie's opinions had weight because she had been welcomed into the household as a person of value, not an object of pity. So, for some thirty years she sat up with the family's sick and its dead.

Meanwhile, in a back room, the children's father talked to the three little girls. His eyes avoided theirs, as he looked at their mother, pregnant and due to deliver within a month. She stood by silently. His words came, low and halting, "Christmas will be different this year. John Albert being so sick and all, Santa Claus won't be..." As his voice trailed away, the youngest girl, only eight, bowed her head. The red-gold curls hid her tears. The middle one, about 10, fixed her dark eyes on the fire and sat very still. The oldest, almost a woman at twelve, encouraged him with her soft gray eyes so like her mother's. She gave him her wide smile that was to win the hearts of all who knew her, tossed her head and said, "We understand. We are not babies!"

Their mother said, "We'd best go on and put away the boxes."

Her husband looked past her into the sick room. There on the old peddle sewing machine were four shoe boxes, all decorated by the kids with ribbon, lace and holly, awaiting whatever Santa might bring.

The father shook his head and began putting on coat, hat and mittens, "Leave them where they are. I'm going to go to the store. I can be back before midnight."

"But, you have no money..." his wife began.

His look silenced her.

"Well, then, don't ride the black mare," she said. "She is so wild and the ground is icy."

He did not answer, just lit his lantern and went to the big barn. He readied the black mare for a trip. She was wild, but she was fast. He reached for the saddle horn to mount up and she made a leap, jerking the reins from his hand. Off she galloped into the blackness. The man raised the lantern and saw Old Bill, a tall raw-boned mule, munching hay in his stall. He saddled the mule and rode back by the house. As he put the lantern on the back porch, his wife came to the door, smiling her approval when she saw he was riding Old Bill. But she knew he wouldn't be making it back by midnight.

After man and mule had gone a mile or so, the man remembered the part about having no money. He rode up to his nearest neighbor's house. After a short conversation with the occupant, a crumpled bill changed hands.

When the pair finally got to town, the man roused the storekeeper from his bed. It seemed that ten dollars bought an amazing amount of stuff this trip—a nice pile of apples, oranges, and candy.

As Old Bill pointed his big ears for home, the man began to fret, "What if John Albert should die before I can get back? I ought to have just let Santa not come this year." He bowed his head and prayer came with difficulty, "Lord spare him, not because he is mine, but that he might be useful to you and his fellow man."

His praying done, he raised his face to the biting wind. Through a break in the rushing clouds, he saw the moon for an instant. The bit of shine lifted his spirits. Old Bill sensed his master's mood and responded by breaking into a lurching gallop. The mule's burst of energy was short-lived. At a saunter, the two finally reached home long past midnight.

In their absence, Grannie had been proved right. John Albert's fever had finally broken and he had been able to sit up in bed.

The father always took the credit, he believed that it was his praying that had done the trick. Not only had the pneumonia been beaten, but his boy's sickly days were finished for good.

My father's notes told no more.

But I know that little John Albert grew up, married my mother (who made him drop that "Albert" part) and had two fabulous daughters—me and Jill. And though he lived a rather ordinary life he was a force for good throughout. Me and my sister have not found anyone who ever heard our Daddy say one single word that wasn't wise or kind or hilarious. Seriously, not a single word was wasted. To our enjoyment, a great many of them were hilarious.

In fact, he was so wise and gave such great advice, me and Jill were thinking about trance channeling him after he died. We haven't gotten around to actually doing it yet. However, very often we just open our mouths without thinking and this fabulous advice comes out. Of course, once in a while it doesn't. Sometimes it's just "Get a better haircut." But that can't hurt.

After the ninth grade, Daddy started going to the big school—Ethel High School. In Attala County, Mississippi. Their big football rival was Kosciusko High—an even bigger school. They probably had 3 or 4 times as many as the forty or so who went to the one in Ethel. One of the good things about going to a real small school is that everybody gets to be something if they want to. For instance, Daddy was six feet tall and weighed 115 pounds and he played football. He was so skinny that when his momma took in his pants (*the* pair of pants), she had to take such a big tuck in the waist til he ended up with one back pocket. The left one completely covered the right one. I do not know what he wore to play football. I don't know if they had pads and hats and stuff. I'm pretty sure they had a ball of some kind because, when we were little, he would sometimes sing us to sleep with, "Cheer, boys, cheer, when Ethel has the ball! We're going to hit that line..." And so on.

By the time I was being schooled, it was already passé to make a kid memorize much of anything. So I didn't. They were still making you memorize the multiplication tables, so I can recite those, with feeling, if called upon. We would call upon our Daddy, or not, and he would belt out stuff about October's bright blue weather, and one-if-by-land, and about tales told by idiots being full of sound and fury signifying nothing. I had not minded any of this, so I figured I could put up with a poetry reading. Provided I had a drink.

Our friend Dix did not look pleased about the prospect of having poems read to him. Drinks or not. Plus they didn't have his favorite, Dixie Beer what else, on hand.

Hiram the Scot said, "I am surprised they didn't mention the poetry reading part to you because they are really, really excited and thrilled to have two famous poets on the campus. And especially to have them here at this private party."

I suggested that we probly ought to get on out of there before they actually commenced the reading part, which looked imminent.

They agreed and we turned to head back through the swinging door, with Dix leading the way. He stopped short, right in the doorway, and we sort of bumped up against his substantial beer-slinging back. He blocked our progress with one meaty paw on the door and the other fumbling in his pants pocket for something. My cringe was pure reflex. But needless. In a flash he whipped out a little round box, about the size of a Dannon yogurt. He sort of rotated it in the air, like he was shaking up the contents and held it up and out toward the folks on the floor of the parlor. And then he hollered out, "HERE'S WHAT I THINK OF Y'ALL AND YOUR POEMS!!!"

From the little round box in his hand came a loud series of chortles, snorts, chuckles, titters, guffaws—lots of guffaws, giggles and snickers and all manner of merriment. And it went on for a good little while. Then Dix shook the thing in the air again and another cheery chorus ensued.

I guess he'd spent part of his day gainfully occupied at some bar room claw machine. We stared at some twenty-five or thirty mouths, flopping open in one enormous gasp of dismay. Me and that ex-husband hurled ourselves against Dix and pushed out the front door. We formed a chorus with the laff box as we ran down the stairs and into the night. As we clasped our sides and gasped for breath, Dix announced that he was real glad he had chosen the box that laughed instead of the one that mooed.

After a while, I said to that X, "So, you knew about the poets, didn't you?"

"They did mention something about them, but I forgot. Until we ran into Dix. Then I remembered," he answered.

"So, why in the world did you drag Dix there?"

"Well," he rejoined smartly, "I knew that somebody was gonna to have to jack with 'em and I thought it would be better if Dix did it instead of me. Then you could be mad at him—instead of me. Plus, I didn't even know about the laff box."

"For your future reference, I do like it better when you are an asshole-by-proxy!"

Ferlinghetti came to town recently, but I didn't go see him. Why mess with an already perfect memory?

That ex-husband rarely took my suggestion of asshole-by-proxy. We could have used Dix again on the occasion of one of the Tulane University football games. A big gang of us would meet up and sit together in the north end zone. It was so high up you couldn't see the game very well, but there were other considerations. Like having plenty of room to lounge about. And spread out the picnic. Sometimes we'd bring bar supplies as well.

This was about the time the stadium people experimented with their method of selling beer to fans. Instead of having guys walking around with those wire carriers full of cups of beer, they invented the back-pack. It was a big ole tank full of beer. The vendor wore it on his back. It had a long thin hose with a hand-held dispenser on the end by which cups could be filled with lots of foam and hardly any beer for a whole lot of money. It was very cunning. That X thought those beer tanks were the cutest things.

So, on this night we parked at his tavern, and prepared to stroll on over to Tulane for the ball game, like always. "Hold on a minute," he said. "I need to run inside for something." In a flash he was back.

"Look what I found?!!" he beamed proudly as he stuck a very shiny, very big beer tank in my face.

"Where in the hell did you get that?"

"I found it. Really," he insisted mulishly.

"What are you going to do with it?" I wondered worriedly.

"It's for the game, of course, whaddya think?"

"For the game?"

"Yes, I came by here this afternoon and filled it all up with beer and I've cups all ready and everything. It holds a lot!" he said gleefully.

"How are you going to get it there?"

"I'm going to wear it, of course, whaddya think?" as he began to put the thing on. He slung it around behind him and hooked his arms through the harness, just like a backpack. He had the dispenser in his hand, waving it to and fro like a scepter.

Then he eagerly made to draw me a cool one.

"That's okay, I'll wait til we get there. But thanks," I said

"Isn't this great!" he sang

"Just swell," I agreed. "But how are you going to get it past security? You know they confiscate all outside booze they can find anyway. Plus they will surely recognize this tank as a piece of their very own equipment."

"Don't worry. I thought of that," he told me smugly.

He went over to his car and opened the door to the back seat. He dug around on the floor among the ankle-deep trash. In a minute he hit paydirt. He pulled something out of there, I couldn't tell what. He shook it out and I saw that it was his really nasty, formerly tan, formerly London Fog, formerly nice trench coat.

"Voila!" said he.

"Yeh, voy-la," I responded.

He struggled and wrestled with the coat. I pitched in and helped make it go around him and the beer tank. I stood on a chair to get better leverage and gave it a real good yank to get the collar up over the top of the beer tank. Since the tank extended about a foot above the top of his head, it was more like a trench jacket than a trench coat. It covered the whole tank, but only came down to about mid-butt. And the sleeves were hiked way up, above his elbows. Ridiculous.

And off we went.

Along the way to the stadium, we encountered clumps of fellow fans. But, as it happened, no one we knew. Everyone stared and stared. And laughed, after we passed them. We were moving quickly, in spite of that ex-husband's extra burden. Because he couldn't wait to get there and show off his new toy to the gang in the north end zone. He slowed down to fish out our tickets and hand them over to me, "You do the talking," he urged. "Then they won't notice."

"I agree that I look especially fetching this evening. But, believe me, they are going to notice. You should see yourself," I cackled.

"Maybe not," he insisted stubbornly. Just because he'd been able to get that dog Jason into the stadium that time, he was more sure of himself than he ought to have been. But Jason had been able to take off running and he could run up under things. I did not think that ex-husband would be able to do that with that big ole tank on his back. Although, he was real strong. If highly motivated he probly could run pretty fast with the thing.

There was no use at all arguing with him. Once he'd set a course, he was bound to carry it out, if it hare-lipped the devil. I had two choices: A) Go along, or B) Not go along.

Since we were almost at the stadium entrance, I chose A) Go along. Besides, I was, by now, pretty entertained by the whole thing. I, too, wanted see what the gang in the north end zone thought. Even though I seriously doubted that they would ever get to see the tank. I figured the first security guy we hit at the gate would A) confiscate the tank, B) arrest that ex-husband, or C) both. I had resolved that I would not be penalized in anyway myownself.

That X guided us to one of the less popular gates. There was nobody in line. In fact, nobody there but us. Apart from the one security guy. I gave him the tickets and a big grin, while trying to lock eyes and keep him from looking at the idiot next to me. The guy smiled pleasantly, took the tickets, and then—looked at the idiot next to me.

"Well, well. What do we have here?" asked the security guard, softly, but still smiling.

That ex-husband took a friendly step forward, sticking out his hand for a shake, "What we have here, sir, is a hunchback," he said cheerfully.

Right there is where I fell against the concrete wall of the concourse, in order to devote myself to a good howl. The security guard started howling too! Weep fest. And, like I said, nobody was around. So, he let us in. I was so impressed and I told that ex-husband so. Every now and then, you've just got to give an asshole his due.

Right here is why I loved that man: he said, "Much as I'd like to let you think that I am so slick and so lucky—and you know how much I love for you to think that?" he said looking deeply into my eyes.

I nodded slowly.

"Yes, much as I'd like that—and I could let you go on thinking that, because you would never know otherwise."

I nodded some more, *otherwise* is something I often didn't know. Sometimes I'll just believe anything.

"Well, missy," he said, "Much as I hate to disabuse you of your faith in me. I must confess that that friendly handshake I gave that guard contained my even friendlier fifty-dollar-bill!"

Me and that X both loved to tell the beer tank story, except the fifty-dollar-bill part. It's more fun to pretend that the guard played along because he got into the spirit of the thing.

So the gang in the north end zone got to see the tank. They were sitting way up high so they could see that X coming for a good long way. In spite of the clever disguise, they quickly discerned that he was wearing a beer dispenser on his back. They began to howl. And then to applaud. And to stand and applaud and cheer. And the surrounding clumps of fans began to howl and applaud and stand and applaud, all pea-green with envy. That X responded to the adulation with a small twinkling smile. In his vast repertoire, this really was modest.

Loosening the Ties That Bind

As a freshly-minted ex-wife, I leased quarters that were short on charm, but long on view. Cutest Guy in The World and his silver Ferrari were right next door. Sweet Inspiration. Not only for me, but for that nephew who had just begun styling around the girls. Our new neighbor set a fine example in both the quantity and quality departments. And his overall demeanor toward women was a lot more conventional than that ex-husband's. I was glad for that nephew to have some exposure to the way regular guys act. Plus, I had blown my wad in the "Helpful hints for young men" department. However, the little bit of advice I had been able to give was dandy, if I do say so myself. I told him that young women were really not as different from young men as he might imagine. In spite of the fact that they went about acting real different. I told him that I believed that healthy young women are every bit as eager to fool around as the guys are.

"They are just about as trashy as ya'll are," I assured him. However, I urged, nay exhorted him to keep all social interaction he might be so fortunate as to enjoy in strictest confidence. "Because, you see, they want to do stuff but they don't want anyone to know about it. You should not tell *anyone, anything, ever*," I explained to him. "While you are standing around being close-mouthed, there will be a fair amount of lip flapping going on among the wimmen. News that your credo is 'Shut My Mouf' will get around. That tired business about strong, silent types? Think silent. Strong is strictly an afterthought. Keep quiet and shortly your opportunities for social interaction will be quite bountiful. Furthermore, this plan will stand you in good stead your whole life long."

That nephew has thanked me profusely through the years. In fact, he has often said this was the best advice anyone ever gave him. That just tickled me to death.

One day I returned home from endless annoying errands to find the big brown convertible hulking in front of my door. In fact, it was in the space that I had come to regard as my spot. I peered into the car just in case that ex-husband and the brown dog were crouched down in the there. It would have been no surprise, albeit startling, to find myself the brunt of a bit of "Pop! Goes the Asshole!" With a free-range X and his faithful, furry companion anything was possible.

The car was empty. I wondered who they might be visiting on my block and hoped it wasn't the Cute Guy. I had gotten to be pretty good friends with him but I hadn't told him all that much about my past. I wasn't trying to keep anything a secret it was just that experience had taught me that there were no words to adequately prepare people for the reality of that ex-husband. I had long ago learned that full-blown descriptions merely brought on accusations of exaggeration or even malice.

What I still think is pretty funny is that when I first met that X, I didn't notice anything much about him, except that he was a big guy who talked a little different. He seemed even bigger than he actually was because he wore actual winter clothing, which was very bulky. Some southerners don't even own a winter coat. His accent was merely Tidewater Virginia, but did stand out a bit amongst the other shades of southern. He and the tennis player from Australia were the most different sounding guys at our rural university.

Actually, it was pretty amazing that that ex-husband was there at all. He barely made it in—on a Governor's Decree. He had some less than cordial relationships with a couple of other institutions of higher learning. He had, as usual, waited til past the cut-off date to apply for admission to this one. His father called in a wad of favors and got his friend the Governor to use up one of his special admissions decrees to get him in. He turned up in two of my classes because, after three years of college and a very busy social schedule, he was still finishing up some freshman stuff.

Alphabetical accident did not seat us together, but soon he was sitting by me all the time. I didn't notice at first because I was busy thinking about myself. I was nice and friendly to him, like I was to everyone. Like all southern girls were and pretty much still are. In a little bit, he asked for my phone number. I still didn't notice. I thought it was because of class assignments and so on. We didn't have any of the same friends. He drove this raggedy-ass old Buick convertible and lived off campus in an equally raggedy-ass apartment house known as the Goat Castle. I did not have a thought in the world of joining the party at the Goat Castle, which went on practically non-stop.

He began chatting me up about finding him a date and I agreed to do that. It proved to be impossible. I soon found that a lot of girls had heard about this guy. He had a hideous reputation. He would take a girl out and then in a little bit he'd get bored or aggravated with her and he'd go off and leave her stranded wherever they happened to be at the time. The girl would have to hustle up a ride home, which was not always that easy since the university didn't have a big town for a hub. I don't remember ever seeing a taxicab. The recreational spots frequented by the students were far flung. And it seemed like he was guilty of even worse stuff that wasn't spelled out—just alluded to in shocked tones. Clearly, this was a bad seed. When he phoned up to get the name of his date, I was in a quandary. I was so embarrassed for him. What a waste of good empathy. Little did I know, this guy hadn't been embarrassed about anything since the fourth grade.

"I didn't have time to find you a date for this weekend," I told him.

"Why don't you go with me?" he asked. "You already said that you're not doing anything Friday night."

This was very unusual because, not only was I cute as I could be, there were about a dozen guys for every girl at our school. It was very difficult not to have a lot of dates.

If my life were set to music, this is where the "Jaws" or "Psycho" sounds would tune up in the background. I was approaching an intersection of my life.

"Welllllllll..." I couldn't bring myself to tell him outright that I couldn't go out with a guy like him. Or that I didn't want to. Convention dictated that no candidate was so offensive that you were allowed to tell him the truth.

"Oh, come on," he wheedled. "You don't want to sit in the dorm on a Friday night. Folks'll think you're losing your touch, Miss Three Dates in One Day."

"Well, so what?" I really could juggle going out with three different guys in one day: one would take me to the brunch before the football game, another to the football game, and yet another would escort me to the party after the game. And they all three would know about the schedule and not object. Each felt mighty lucky to have any time with me at all. Perfect. If this kind of thing didn't get a body to acting all biggitty-speckle, then I guess nothing would. However, it's prudent to be mindful. Biggitty-speckle goeth before the fall. It's perfectly fine to do some prancing. But if you start taking yourself seriously, that's when you might find yourself easing over into that treacherous biggity-speckle area. And you're just begging the universe for some come-uppance.

If a woman is ever sitting around bored and thinking that life is just sooooooo perfect, I'll tell you how she can find some exciting bumps in the road. All she has to do is draw up and point the finger at that woman over there who's having romance troubles. And then she should say "Well, I sure wouldn't put up with that from any man. That girl should have used better judgment in her choices." True though this probably is, it guarantees who the next woman with the problem is going to be.

Comeuppance watching is big fun. Comeuppance receiving ain't. Avoid it.

"So, how about Friday night?" he continued.

I mustered my nerve, such as it was. "I don't know," I said. "I hear stuff and I heard that you ditch your dates!"

"*I am not in the habit of abandoning women I ask out,*" he said. I would one day learn that this pomposity was what his impersonation of his father sounded like.

The first time I met the Dad, he was passing through the state on his way back to D.C. and paused to take his eldest child to dinner. By then, I was the designated "Main Squeeze" and invited to come along. I also discovered that I was the designated buffer between a father and son who held each another in complete contempt. That Dad conversed the entire time in tones plenty loud enough to be heard by each and every person in the restaurant. By the time he was done, they all thought he was a

U.S. Senator. Which is exactly what he wanted them to think. It was, "Senator Kennedy this and my friend Justice Burger that," and blah, blah, blah. It was embarrassing and real boring. It would have been all right if we could all play. Shoot, we could all be senators or ambassadors or something. But he was only interested in a solo act.

The man had a perfectly respectable job as a lawyer for the Senate, so he did know lots of influential types in Washington, or "The District." And he was called upon many, many times to use these contacts, which he freely did, to bail his offspring out of scrapes. Which he should not have done. And I think he missed the father of the year award by a wide margin on account of he used memos as his main mode of communicating with his children. He used those tear-apart forms—original to the kid, copy to the file. Never a phone call, except when the aforementioned scrapes came up. I guess it's a wonder that ex-husband wasn't a worse critter than he was. God knows why I ever hooked up with him. Well actually, God knows and so do I. I confused defective with exotic.

Our families didn't look all that different from the outside. You couldn't tell by looking what was going on in the parenting department. I think in his case nothing much. In mine, the touch was so light and so deft, I didn't much notice the reins.

My family agreed that one of the lowest things a body could do was to envy somebody else's stuff. Our deal was that stuff in general was worthless until we bestowed ownership on it. No need to give a thing a thought until it belongs to you, then you can right away notice that it is wonderful.

We learned about envy from when we were real small from the "Black Cat Bone" story—the lore of black and white folks alike. The recipe was fairly simple.

1 solid black cat without a single white hair

Boil for three days

Somehow that last part was glossed over. But a single, shiny bone would remain. I imagined it would look like a picked clean baby back rib.

The deal was you put the black cat bone in your pocket and it made you invisible. Our Daddy swore that one time this man named Zeke bought such a bone from a fortune teller. Zeke had worked many years for a rich man named Whitlock, in Attala County, as a valued and trusted employee.

However, way down deep, Zeke was one seriously dissatisfied man. He had a big weakness. He coveted his neighbors' stuff. All of his neighbors and all of their stuff. And the thing he coveted most in the world was Mr. Whitlock's gold pocket watch with the fancy fobs. He wanted that watch in the worst way. He dreamed about it night and day. Zeke saw himself out front of the church on Sunday mornings. He'd pull that watch out like he was checking the time, turning it this way and that way to catch the sunlight, setting those fobs a-shining. But Zeke hardly ever cared what time it was.

It wasn't like Zeke didn't have a nice life. He had a nice wife and nice children and a nice house and a job he liked working for a man who liked him. He even had a watch. But he never carried it, because, like I said, Zeke hardly ever cared what time it was.

To Zeke his own stuff and his own life just didn't seem all that shiny. It all seemed to fade or shrink or wrinkle or something when he compared it to the other fellow's.

Now Zeke had his Black Cat Bone. He was not studying on slipping around town, performing anonymous good deeds. That very night, after his wife went to sleep, he put the bone in his pocket and went to the Whitlock house. They were all asleep over there, too. Zeke went right in because nobody locked their doors. They had long ago misplaced their keys.

He went straight to Mr. Whitlock's bedroom. He spied the watch on the dresser, gleaming in the moonlight. Zeke snatched it up, causing the fobs to jingle. The Whitlock's woke and sat up in the bed.

"Zeke, what in hell are you doing in here?" queried Whitlock.

Zeke answered promptly, "Why, you can't see me! I've got a Black Cat Bone."

There was no more story, but family conversation continued. About how Zeke had shamed himself and his family. Zeke had a good thing going and just went and let his envy mess it all up.

My raising wasn't perfect or anything, I just don't think a kid learns much from a memo. Except who to call to get him outta jail.

So, ummmm.... Oh, yeah, I was there in front of my bachelorette place. I turned from that ex-husband's empty car and I went on inside. I was stunned to behold that ex-husband and the brown dog leisurely scrounging through my stuff. Of course, I know that the real surprise was that I was still stunable.

"Don't worry," that ex-husband cheerfully assured me, as he paused from browsing my mail, "We didn't have to break in or anything."

"I am so glad you weren't put to any trouble, but since there's no chimney, exactly how...?"

"Oh. Well, you see your locksmith just happens to be my locksmith, too. And he just happened to have an extra key," he matter-of-facted over his shoulder as he went on pyrooting my mail. (*py·root, v. Cajun.* to f--- with somebody else's stuff; to rummage.)

I looked to that space in my heart reserved for pissed-off and found instead grudging admiration for the biggest brass balls I had ever encountered. (Or even better, like writer Rivka Solomon says, "That Takes Ovaries.")

My reaction, and a thousand others just like it, accounts, in part, for the number of years I'd stayed married to this incorrigible.

I reached in my purse for one of the spare keys I had just that minute come from having made at the hardware store, "I got this for you—in case of emergency—with that nephew living here and the brown dog visiting and all," I deadpanned.

You could hear the crest falling. Permission sure can spoil the fun.

I had planned all along to give that ex-husband a key. My privacy was not much at risk for I planned to live a demure life as long as that nephew was in my home.

Me and that nephew had settled into our new routine and had enjoyed several months of hum-drum, a pleasant novelty for us. Then, one pre-dawn I was jolted into pre-consciousness by loud barking and bell ringing and door pounding.

"Who could it be?" I wondered. I guessed right off that it was probably not the Cute Guy from next door. Although we had gone around together some, he was way younger than me. But had turned out to be a good running buddy. There had been one particularly satisfying outing. We started out together on a gorgeous fall afternoon, riding around in that sporty car of his—the silver Ferrari. Since the day was so fine, a lot of folks were outside playing and they got to see me having a great time with one of the best looking guys alive. As anyone who's ever been a petty, shallow person like I am knows: nothing much beats this.

But, no o o o o, it sure wasn't the Cute Guy at my door. It was my own personal dynamic duo. That ex-husband and the brown dog were on their way to take in a sunrise and they were looking for company. How courteous of them to knock. Perhaps they had forgotten their key.

"Get the hell outta my yard," I snarled through lips pressed against the jamb of the door, which was both closed and dead-bolted.

"She's sometimes cranky like this when she first wakes up," he remarked to the brown dog. "We just need to persuade her."

Their idea of cajolery was to seize the solid oak church pew decorating my front porch and use it to bust open my front door.

"So, as long as you're up, why don't you come on and go up to look at the river with us?" he wheedled. Many times we had driven through Audubon Park, behind the zoo, to sit and watch the Mississippi River and the traffic on it. It was very hypnotic and soothing. I would mouth-breathe contentedly, but he didn't know how. He was able to sit quietly for only about two or three minutes and then he'd be tapping on the steering wheel. Then he'd be starting with the jimmy-leg. It took me a few years with him to get to where I could maintain a trance with all that wiggling and squirming going on beside me.

Just now, I was not interested in being soothed, so I snatched up the phone and punched 9ll. In one big scurry, they were out through the now gaping doorway, into the big brown convertible, and around the corner in a cloud of cinders.

I replaced the receiver—no one had answered any-way—nailed the door shut and went back to bed, fuming over this fresh hell. That nephew never even woke up and neither did any of the neighbors. Just as well, in a way. Any chance to save some embarrassment. But, it reinforced what I'd been knowing for a while: Honey, you are on your own! It also confirmed that me and that ex-husband had been having way too much contact because of our continuing business partnership.

Since I was handling the advertising and public relations, and more recently the entertainment bookings for our night club, we had lots of meetings. Furthermore, I found that booking part to be the hardest thing I'd ever done in my life. I didn't know jack about music or musicians or records or tapes or CD's or sound equipment. Even still to this day, I remain on the cutting edge of ignorance. My lack of knowledge did not make me so uncomfortable that I cared to study up or anything, it just made me real jumpy and crabby. I don't mind being stupid but I don't care for looking stupid. Plus, I got involved in this booking stuff just at a time when, nationally, the music business was going through a near-death experience. Record company promotional funding dried up so the artists quit going on tour.

Even though New Orleans never had been a for-sure stop on the tours like the major markets were, entertainers loved coming here. They'd come to town for the food and the fun and stop by and see us. And to see local stars like the Meters, Deacon John, Irma Thomas, Professor Longhair, Willie T, The Copas Brothers, Lil Queenie, The Cold, The Radiators, the subdudes, The Rhapsodizers, Gatemouth Brown, or Clifton Chenier. One time Paul and Linda McCartney and Wings came to our place to see the Neville Brothers, two shows. Another time, a bunch of folks from *Rolling Stone* magazine were hanging out. We had a group from south Louisiana playing. They were excellent musicians and the "Stone" people wanted to adopt them and take them to L.A. and make them really big stars. But the band took a vote among themselves and unanimously rejected the offer. They had already played at a few places "away" and they didn't much care for getting too far from home. What musical riches we had—still have.

If I do say so myownself, I had done a fair job of getting our little venue steady bits of national press. So when that ex-husband was arranging for the artists, he got lots of big people to add a New Orleans gig to their tours. He'd been able to get folks like Ry Cooder and Taj Mahal and Eddie Money and the Paul Butterfield Blues Band and Muddy Waters and Kinky Friedmann and Guy Clark and Ray Wiley Hubbard and Larry Raspberry and the Hi-Steppers and Darryl Rhoades and the HaHa Vishnu Orchestra and Delbert McClinton—I think we might have loved Delbert even before Don Imus! And he got Elvis Costello and Ronee Blakely and John Prine and Leon Redbone and Meatloaf. Meatloaf never actually did the gig because the neighborhood bar rabble harassed him during the afternoon sound check (more music lingo). Mr. Loaf got a case of the red angst and said they weren't going to play. That ex-husband's skilled public relations response to this was, "Well fine then. *Get out.*"

One time right before he was headed out of town, that ex-husband hired these three guys (Sonny, Terry and Brownie McGhee) as the main act. I knew they were "Somebody" cause they cost a lot. I needed to find an opening act right quick so I signed up one of the many local new wave punk rock bands. The night of the performance was when I found out that what we had was a *duo*: Sonny Terry and Brownie McGhee—two bona fide legends in the world of blues. I came this close to demanding to know why our third guy hadn't showed up. In addition, one of them was blind and I never did find out which one. I did learn that the two hated each other's guts and would only communicate through me. The brown dog hated both their guts and was dying to do some ass-chewing. He thought it would be a great help to his own personal case of the blues.

After I was able to get the brown dog secured-away from the bickering musicians, I couldn't think of anything to say to smooth things over. I wouldn't have been able to think of anything to say even if they hadn't been bickering. I could not speak musician at all and could understand only a smattering. When they weren't on stage, I spent my time relaying their gripes and insults back and forth between them. If I hadn't been so nervous, it would have been much funnier. Even I was able to grasp the incongruity of the blues guys and the punk rockers. This was a night that needed getting over with. The punk rockers were thrilled to bits for this unexpected opportunity to open for someone famous. And Sonny and Brownie, though awful to each other, were nothing but gracious to the wannabe rockers.

Later that same week, a music critic in the local paper gave the evening a great review. He said it had been "A daring and innovative pairing of musical styles—a real coup!" Get outta town.

I decided to quit while I was ahead and begin to seek in earnest: A Real Job.

The first thing I did was talk to a couple of people I knew who had real jobs to see if they were tired of them and wanted me to have them or if they knew of any spare jobs. Sure enough, one did. This is the way we mostly get jobs in New Orleans. I have sometimes wondered how other folks do it. Also what sometimes happens here is that while a person is doing this employment research, their parents will hire them or get one of their friends to. My friend sent me to see this pair of really cute guys, both named John. They were in the beverage business—Barq's Root Beer, Barq's Creme Soda and Delaware Punch. Since the root beer had been around for about a hundred years and sold like hot cakes in the deep south, I had actually heard of it. And I had an historical connection to it. One of my relations had owned the franchise rights in Jackson, Mississippi. A great, great uncle had been the attorney for old man Barq who had first invented the root beer. Mr. Barq had bartered for the legal services and promised the guy 5 cents a case for every case of the stuff sold in the state of Mississippi. I didn't know any of this at the time of the interview.

Me and the Johns had a pleasant chat and I was made to feel very comfortable. So much so that when they asked me why I wanted to work for them, I responded briskly, "I am still in a business partnership with that ex-husband and we work so closely that everybody thinks I'm still married to him and it's interfering with my social life."

To their everlasting credit, they thought that this was a dandy reason to be seeking employment. And to my own credit, I have elected not to cringe with embarassment every time I think about my saying that. Thus began a long and happy relationship. I was able to utilize my fairly nebulous talents to our mutual benefit. After I got to know them a bit better, I began demanding the 5 cents per case deal that had been in effect with my relations in olden days. I could not sell them on this plan, but my compensation package was quite generous.

As soon as I began to make decent money, that ex-husband began whining, "So can I quit paying you that alimony now that you have a real job?"

"Certainly not," I responded firmly.

"Well, okay then," he agreed.

Now I did my very best to make him feel good about those alimony payments. Like whenever I bought a new car I'd rush right over to take him for a ride in it: "See, this is what I use that alimony money for. This is what your money pays for—it's not like I'm wasting it or anything. This is your money at work." And he would nod happily.

Taking a Meeting

THE CORNERSTONE OF MY PROPERTY SETTLEMENT in the divorce was the Lifetime Bar Tab: I got free-stuff-in-perpetuity at the night spots that ex-husband continued to operate after we split up. Plus, I would get to horn in on any new ventures—in this modest way. Although, some people would not consider the bills associated with my socializing all that modest. I also had "taking over" privileges which were not as defined, but just as highly prized. This meant that I could just arrive and take over and everyone had to do what I said.

There were many places where this had been known to happen purely by chance, especially when Jill and I were together. We could wax formidable if we were in the mood. One time we went out dancing just after a stint in Cozumel. We were all brown which we love because we haven't any sense. Especially me, as I am a blue-eyed blonde. Although we had fried to about the same doneness, Jill looked darker because of her dark hair and eyes.

We took to the dance floor, hollering in "Spanish" and trying to take up all the room. We thought everyone loved us and life was just grand. We were not wearing any underwear and were doing lots of jumping around. We were stunning.

Meanwhile, seated at the bar was the late poet and colorful character, Everett Maddox. (He was not late right then.) He asked the bartender, "Who is that Mexican woman who's making Judy act up like that?" It was all my seester's fault!

When we were done dancing, we headed to that ex-husband's club so we could get free stuff. After we had gotten quite a bit of free stuff, we went to the bathroom. While Jill made faces at herself in the mirror, I was in one of the stalls reading aloud to her from the graffitti. As you'd guess, the accoustics were good and so I read with verve. A lot of the material was naturally directed at that ex-husband, since he was well-known as the owner of the place. And then there was his renown among those who might frequent the ladies room. I read with relish that Kay T. "hates the owner's guts" and that F.D., Gretchen, and Little Bit always "call him for a good time." And on to how he "comes in his tightie whities" and "sucks little green donkey dicks."

We were pretty tickled from the refreshments and the urban literature. Since me and Jill are literary and way more fun than the Bronte sisters, we decided that we were duty-bound to contribute some sally to the wall liberry. We have always wanted to "write something together," so we were gleeful at the prospect. I said, "Sh-h-h-h. If we write it in here, he'll know it was us. Everyone saw us come in here. Let's sneak upstairs to the other bathroom. Then, he'll never know."

So, off we snuck. Sly boots we were, skulking around the edges of the crowd. We made our way upstairs. "I don't think anyone saw us," Jill whispered. Not that anybody at all was particularly watching for us—but we are just naturally pretty hard to miss.

Eyeliner pencils in hand, we prepared to create. It took us a little while because we kept dropping our writing utensils. Then we saw a line that said "The owner of this place is a pig." Whereupon we added what would logically follow, "yeah and he eats oink-boogers." Due to there being something in the water, our mental age was temporarily five and we thought this was one of the funniest things we ever did. We still do. We don't think it was in any way lame.

The very next day, I got a drop-by from that ex-husband. Imagine my delight upon being informed that he was thinking about being a partner in a new deal. A couple of guys wanted him to come in with them on a night club inside the grounds of the New Orleans World's Fair & Exposition. La-dee-dah. What immediately sprang to my mind were images of me and my friends having a much nicer place to hang out and drink free in.

And perhaps there would be some people from somewhere else, or at least some who were not kin to people we know.

Now, right here is where I demonstrated, yet again, what a stand-up ex-wife I was. Putting all these personal considerations aside, I spoke right up.

"*Have you lost your mind?*" I snorted. "I know you've lost your memory. You already lost a big old wad of money in a deal with one of those guys. They do not intend to make any money. They hardly ever make any money. They might lose tons of money on paper for tax purposes and other assorted boondoggles, but they will lose some actual money. And that's where you come in, you sap. You will be providing the money they will actually lose. And besides that, they hate your guts."

"I know all that," he countered. "But this thing is going to be real fun and I want to do it anyway and I don't care if I do lose money."

"Well, that's different. Just don't come whining to me."

As you might imagine, other approvals besides mine were required before that ex-husband would be a bona fide partner. A crucial meeting was scheduled in the boardroom of a bank. This in no way implied that the bank was endorsing the World's Fair. No indeedy. They did not have to take a very good look to determine that it was a loser. However, it was far too dignified an institution to engage in warning folks away. They stood by, as always, ever eager to open that savings account for you. Meanwhile, naive and opportunity-starved locals mortgaged their homes and looted college funds to jump on a bandwagon that was top-heavy with under-capitalized suckers and on a collision course with financial reality.

That ex-husband had been in his spring training program for some weeks by that time. This entailed his getting up most everyday in time to catch a couple of hours of midday sun—supplemented by the lamps at the New Orleans Athletic Club. So come meeting day, he was tan and he was ready. He was not, however, rested. Prior to anything important, he liked to stay up all night in order to achieve that blood-shot-wild-eyed look that he felt gave him a certain edge during any negotiations. He donned his cut-offs. They were faded and shapeless and still salty from the previous weekend spent on the beach over in Bay St. Louis.

Like a lot of New Orleanians, we spent a lot of time on the Mississippi Gulf Coast. We did not have a weekend home there, but our good friends the Higgins did and they just loved for us to bring that nephew and come on over. We would loll around in the sun, drinking screwdrivers, greasing up with Bain de Soleil and Popeye's chicken and listening to oldies on the radio. Folks here are even still slow to turn loose of a musical era. Stuff from the fifties still gets plenty of airplay.

Long about mid-afternoon on Sunday, we'd head back to town, usually stopping for early dinner at some pizza place. I'm not sure what the Higgins did when they got home, but we'd do it in the shower. We had perfected the standing up position and it was possibly our favorite. There is nothing like a cool shower on tight, sunburned skin—while doing it, of course.

For his meeting in the boardroom, that ex-husband donned his shades and stuck a big ole smelly cigar between his teeth—it won out over the toothpick. His going-to-the-bank ensemble was complete. The brown dog was ready, too. He and that ex-husband had had a long shower together their ownselves, as they did most every day. Not as fun as our showers, but nice all the same. Both were anointed tastefully with just a splash of bay rum, their favorite man-made fragrance. Naturally, the brown dog preferred the natural essence of eau de dead squirrel.

The day was a fine one, so they put the top down on the big brown convertible, which you may recall was about the size of a yellow school bus with an exhaust to match. Not your environmental quiet-ride. They took the scenic route, as we all do whenever we can, down St. Charles Avenue. We never get tired of this, the most beautiful street in the world to us. It is a damn good thing those butt-in preservationists butted in when they did or these wonderful old homes would have gone the way they did in my hometown, Jackson, Mississippi. I love Jackson, but they sure were short on butt-in preservationists when they needed some because they tore down a passel of houses to put up Tote-Sums. Folks there are bad about thinking you just can't have too many convenience stores. But my Daddy, Mississippi born and bred, who found as many ways as a human could to make life more convenient, managed just fine without ever finding it necessary to venture inside of a single convenience store. Jackson is just plain bad about building new stuff and deserting the old stuff, which shortly becomes the ugly stuff. They've got dozens of ugly shopping malls that no one goes to anymore.

Neither that ex-husband nor the brown dog was wearing any shoes, so the bank's marble floors were cool on their calloused feet. The tellers stopped mid-count to gaze at the two brown bodies sauntering beneath the soaring ceiling of that hallowed hall. Several chins fell lower than their usual slack-jawed position assumed during business hours in New Orleans. And we do so like a really cheezy summer suit, but preferably the afore-mentioned seersucker. But this guy had dared to come down-town to the main office of the bank without so much as a tank top and flip flops. The bank people hadn't thought to post one of those "No Shirt, No Shoes, No Service" signs. Not that it would have stopped that ex-husband. "Do Not" did not even register in his mind. And another thing, they were used to get-ting the occasional hand-held poodle, groomed within an inch of its life and arriving in a limousine. But this canine specimen was bold as brass and entirely too... well, brown.

Once the pair entered the elevators and the doors closed, the whole bank was abuzz. They wondered if they should call some-body. But they couldn't think who. Besides, that guy might be the idiot brother-in-law of somebody. We are ate up with idiot brother-in-laws around here. They figure prominently when it comes time to hand out government contracts or political ap-pointments. No one seems to much care, except when you find yourself on the butt end of some action taken by one of 'em. Fortunately, there are usually at least two or three extra folks hired to keep the brothers-in-law under control. This also helps out with our unemployment figures. One of the favorite ways to avenge grievances here is to get one of the brothers-in-law all in a tight at your enemy. You know nothing of aggravation unless you've seen an idiot, in power, in action.

In New Orleans the meanest damn thing one human being can do to another is to "Get their street worked on." This is where you set one or more agencies upon somebody's road to "repair" the road, or stuff under the road. It could be the road where your enemy either lives or works. Whichever would cause the most inconvenience. This will absolutely ruin his life. You can fix it so customers can't get to the guy's business for three or four years. Him and his family will have to park blocks away and haul stuff home for-damn-ever. By the time they get to invite people over for dinner again, nobody will remember who they are. And after the work finally ceases, the topography has been rearranged so that his store, his house, his cars will flood every time it rains longer than ten minutes. I know because I was unlucky enough to purchase a house that was near one owned by somebody who gave grief to a city agency. A lot of grief. Pretty soon afterward, the street was "Fixed." Just the one block suddenly received fancy drains, gutters and sidewalks. No other block for a half a mile in any direction had any of that stuff. None of those other blocks flood either. This block floods almost every time it rains. And it never had, not even once, in the ten years prior to the "Improvements." In addition, I have it on good authority that a lot of the drains in town are fake. There is the heavy metal thing, the grate, then nothing. No sewer pipes at all. About two feet down, solid dirt.

Inside the elevator at the bank, that ex-husband and the brown dog were preening in front of the shiny, brass doors. They thought they were pretty fine looking. This view was not shared by the secretarial sentry guarding the door to the sanctum—the Boardroom. Nor, as it turned out, was it shared by the head honcho and his lackies within the boardroom. The honcho barked that there would be no meeting that day or any other as far as he was concerned. That ex-husband and the brown dog shrugged, about-faced, and returned the way they'd come, pausing only to relight the cigar and have a good scratch. When he gleefully recounted to me the events of the day, that ex-husband acted like he and his sidekick had pulled off a major mogul maneuver. The brown dog was pleased that he'd gotten to go to the big dog's bank. I handed out the usual attaboys. Meanwhile I was thinking, "This deal's dead and I don't really give a rat's ass. Since there is no money in it for me." Although I was kind of sorry to give up the notion of a fine and fancy new place to meet and greet—for free.

The following week that ex-husband phoned up to say, "I'm taking another meeting on that World's Fair deal."

"You're taking a what?" I sniggered.

"That's what they say in L.A.," he sniffed indignantly.

"Yeah, I bet that's what they say in L.A. and you'd know all about that, I suppose."

This meeting was to be held at the home of one of the pro-spective partners in the Fair deal (ha!). That ex-husband wanted that nephew to accompany him since other kids would be there, too. I agreed like I always did, me being the perfect ex-wife and all.

"Good, good, good," he murmured.

Pause... More pausing...

"And?" I queried.

"Uhh h h h h, yeah... Could you come, too?"

"What for?"

"W e e l l l l... The partnership wants to meet my wife and family," he mumbled.

The cackling and hooting and chortling that followed this revelation would be me. "Lemme get this straight," I choke. "You want me to snatch your smoking Virginia ham out of the fire you built down there at that bank last week, don'tcha? You want me to lend you my considerable respectability, not to men-tion personal charm, for an evening of faux-wifery?"

That ex-husband had been born and raised in Virginia and at the right stage of inebriation or in between engaging in acts of moral turpitude, he enjoyed very much referring to himself as a Virginia Gentleman. One year for Mardi Gras, we dressed up like a Colonial Virginia Gentleman and his lady. It was not nearly as much of a stretch for me. We had a lot of fun and tons of tourists took our picture and people we knew shrieked with mirth. The get-up inspired that ex-husband to behave all Mardi Gras day in an uncharacteristic decorous fashion. Until about l0:30 that night, when we had to leave the French Quarter and rush back uptown to the F&M Patio where he could get rid of the get-up before his head exploded from the stress of acting nice.

"Uh, yeah," he continued on the phone. "I really need for you and that nephew to go to this meeting with me."

"Will there be dinner?"

"Yep. Either Clancy's or The Upperline, whoever will take us."

"Will there be gifts?" I wondered hopefully.

"Yes there will," he stated stoutly.

"Deal."

There we were: the cute couple and their cute nephew and their cute brown dog. We went to the meeting and acted real nice.

One of the prospective partners took that ex-husband upstairs while that nephew of his went to hang poolside with the other young folks. The other guy stayed downstairs to grill me. I played the charade that I was still married to that ex-husband and that he was normal.

I did do a good job, if I say so myself. So it was no surprise to me that the partnership came to this erroneous conclusion, as others have done: their new partner was merely a tad eccentric. Well, friends, I can promise you that nothing about that ex-husband could be measured in tads.

On the way home later that night, we talked about the meeting.

"You know," I said, "You've been jacking around with these people for over a year now."

"Actually, it's better than two years," he countered.

"So where do these people think I've been all this time."

"I've been tellin' them that you are shy and like to rest a lot."

The Gentleman's Club

T HAT EX-HUSBAND OF MINE always did love a massage, and you know what they always say: If they can't get it at home... So, he joined the venerable New Orleans Athletic Club, a bastion of fantastic rubs and old world thinking. Of course, it was men only membership. We ladies were invited in for cocktails and dinner only on certain evenings and for the Mardi Gras open house. About once a month I availed myself of what I felt was the best turtle soup in town. It was built on the darkest roux, thick with plenty of lemon and sherry.

The club was marble and heavy mahogany paneling and polished brass and copper and sparkling mirrors and distressed leather and *quiet*. And drinks that made me feel like Lauren Bacall—dry martinis and rob roys and manhattans and old fashioneds. In those days, you could smell the starch in the tablecloths and napkins and livery.

The staff made you feel like they cared for your comfort and pleasure. And if you directed the staff, "If anybody calls, I'm not here." Well, then you weren't. No matter who was calling. Although that ex-husband was a man of many transgressions, he never did subject me to the tell-her-I'm-not-here gambit. In retrospect, I think this was not so much due to his integrity as to his everlasting curiosity about what I had to say. Like Scheherazade always used to say, "Nothing draws a man like a good story. Unless it's a good story and a blowjob."

Generations of New Orleans men, the famous and the notorious, had gone there to be pampered and pummeled and tweaked. Or just to hide out for a few hours to get their stories straight. Some would go there after a night of carousing in the French Quarter to be whipped into shape for that day in court or that board meeting. And there were some who needed the full treatment just to get in good enough shape to go home and face their own families. First, their clothing could be whisked away for a much needed "freshening," or maybe complete laundering and dry cleaning if gutter-wallowing had been the order of the evening. In those extreme cases where key elements of the ensemble had somehow been misplaced, an understanding haberdasher on Canal Street would open his shop early for the club's designated shopper. In very short order, a whole new outfit could be assembled for the day's next event.

The rubber—this is what the masseur was called—would

blast them with the fire hose, washing away any remaining bra-
vado. Then followed the full regime: steam, sauna, scrub, rub
and a couple of hours in the sleep room. They would emerge as
bright and shiny as new pennies and redolent of bay rum. Many
a career, not to mention political butt, was saved by the rubbers
at the club. And the marriages? Too numerous to mention.
Barney, the head rubber, reigned supreme. He'd spent over fifty
years taking care of every kind of government body from Huey
Long's to the Jolly Green Giant's. Huey Long was this governor
who was assassinated. Some folks thought Franklin Roosevelt
helped kill him. Barney used to say, "FDR didn't have nothing
to do with it, but he did steal all his ideas from old Huey."

The Green Giant was District Attorney Jim Garrison, later
a judge and Oliver Stone character in the movie "JFK." New
Orleanians were schismed on that movie. Clay Shaw and Jim
Garrison each had their advocates. Hardly anybody was a fan of
both men. However, everybody is of one mind on conspiracy
theories: love 'em! Even better is the actual conspiring. However, around here that's just called "making a plan."

One time that ex-husband and his friend Seth made a plan.
There was this annoying, whining, quasi-political gaggle which
had been demonstrating or protesting or something over at Tulane University. So that X and Seth got a couple of brickbats
upon which they wrote the initials of the whiney political group.
They snuck on campus and flung the brickbats through some
windows and ran away. They thought this was big fun and told
about it quite a bit. Directly, the FBI sent this undercover agent

over to that ex-husband's tavern. He was not far enough under the cover though, because that ex-husband immediately pegged the guy as some kind of cop—and some kind of deviant. It takes one to know one, I guess. He and Seth wondered how the FBI had gotten on to them for the bricking. I suggested that it might have been because they had hollered to all comers, "Hey, guess what we did??!" And then they saved everybody the trouble of guessing. They were also aggrieved that the FBI had sent them a deviant. I guaranteed them that the FBI did not know that their guy was a deviant.

When the guy came in the tavern for the third time, they bought him some drinks and got him to talking. They were very good at that. In a little bit, he was hollering, "Hey, J. Edgar, Bite me!" Then the agent fetched a condom from the men's room and poured his drinks into it, fashioning a dandy prop to accompany an exotic dance. This he performed with enthusiasm to the incredulity of his fellow patrons. Their God-given aplomb sprang back to life, as somebody lunged for the piano to provide accompaniment. Somebody else swiftly brought forth a camera. In a flash, the G-man came to himself. In another flash, he was seized by panic. In the third, he fled the scene amid howls of "Encore, encore!!" He was never seen again.

One of the bit parts in "JFK" went to Jim Garrison's son Eberhardt, or "Eb" as he was more conveniently known. That nephew hosted a movie premier party in Eb's honor. He was really tickled. There was a horde of squealing fans who wanted Eb to autograph the special plastic cups bearing his likeness. At first, the self-effacing Eb was bemused by the attention and cautiously affixed a tiny signature on a proffered cup or two. But before I'd downed my first glass of wine, he'd begun grandly scrawling his name and asking them, "...and you are...?" Star quality.

Just about everyone in New Orleans longs for stardom. And many secretly believe they are stars. This keeps most of the population from being so very keen on stargazing. (There is some interest in starfucking, which is different.) If you are thinking about yourself all the time, as we here are so very fond of doing, you don't have time to waste on the likes of celebrities. One time I was in line at the deli at Martin Wine Cellar uptown branch. I saw that the group ahead of me was extremely loud and animated. Then I saw that Kim Basinger was sitting alone at a table. They were feverishly trying to get her to notice them as they pretended not to see her. She was busy eating her lunch. Plus, she thought that she was the star in the room and had no earthly idea that there was anything at all to claim her interest. Incidentally, Ms. Basinger has lovely skin, but this was not a good hair day.

I've seen rooms full of folks at that X's club turning themselves inside out trying to get Paul McCartney or Bruce Springsteen to watch them. Not a single person would approach the stars for an autograph. A lot of stars like to come to New Orleans so they can go out in public and relax. That's one reason John Goodman likes it here so much.

The folks that hang out in the F&M Patio do like to send

over a drink to a celebrity. And sometimes there is "piling on." That's when everybody and his dog insists on sending a drink over, right now, and the star ends up with about twenty drinks lined up in front of him. But what F&M'ers really like to do is look at themselves in the mirrors behind the bar as they dance atop the pool table.

What that ex-husband liked to do was invite his friends to join him in enjoying the many amenities at the New Orleans Athletic Club. It was only natural that he would want his very best friend to go too. So one day, him and the brown dog piled into the brown convertible and rode, grinning into the wind, downtown to the New Orleans Athletic Club. It was and is located on Rampart Street on the far edge of the French Quarter.

At midday, which was the time of day that ex-husband usually arose to make his toilette, few members were about. By that time, even those few most dedicated of celebrants had gone to tend to their responsibilities. Since the staff never questioned members about anything, the two walked right through the lobby. They went on down the cavernous hallway—the brown dog's nails click, click, clicking on the marble floor, back to the locker room.

By the way, there was enshrined there a marble urinal that, I am told, was as impressive an edifice as any you'd see in Rome. I am also told that one die-hard clubber tried to buy the urinal for use as his headstone in Metairie Cemetery, one of our little cities of the dead. The fancy crypts and mausoleums and, of course, limited acreage, make this some of the most expensive real estate around. Because of the water table and being below sea level—when you're at the River, you look *up* at passing ships—we can't plant our dead. The coffins would just come bubbling out of the ground.

That ex-husband and the brown dog found their spot in front of their locker. One of the pair undressed and then they took a steam together, undisturbed. It was too early in the day for most regulars—about this time, they would just be getting into their liquid lunches real good. I could just see them up in that steam room, sitting side by side with their tongues hanging out. Soon, they'd both be panting like, well, dogs. Next came the rub by Barney. He made no reference at all to the brown dog, watching and dozing in the dim light.

They finished off the afternoon with a swim in the indoor pool. They were frolicking and dog-paddling with abandon when they were joined by the club's chairman of the board. His large, shiny, white, buck-naked self was huffing and puffing through the first lap when he happened to glance to his right and see that the adjoining lane was occupied by the brown dog. He was naked as he could be, too, and grinning sociably. Mr. Board Chairman was quite the spoil-sport. He couldn't get out of the water fast enough.

Upon hauling himself out, he began bellowing about fleas and dog hair and *mange!* The scene at poolside was mighty ugly. By this time, that ex-husband and the brown dog had also gotten out of the pool. That ex-husband, never one to hold his tongue anyway, was very defensive where the brown dog was concerned.

Especially in this situation, since he and the brown dog show-ered together daily. He knew themselves to be both flea and mange-free. Insults were traded, threats made.

Mr. Board Chairman was very lucky that things never got beyond posturing and blustering, for that ex-husband was a vet-eran of countless barroom brawls. I could personally bear wit-ness to his beating the snot out of scores of "malcontents." One time I saw him knock this man clean out of his shoes with one punch. The guy ended up sitting and sniveling on the curb in front of the shoes, still parallel parked just as they'd been when he was in them. It was also a wonder to me that the brown dog didn't chomp a bit of chairmanly butt. His reputation as a taster of human flesh was well known. A small crowd gathered to watch, but not a soul laughed at two bare-assed men and a wet, brown dog—all snarling. I'm wondering what exactly *would* make this bunch enjoy a chuckle.

The upshot of the whole deal was that by the next day that ex-husband was also an ex-member of the New Orleans Athletic Club.

A couple of his la-dee-dah friends used up some favors, pooled their clout, twisted some arms and got him back in with very little delay. But it was never the same. The tight-asses had just ruined it for him. That ex-husband went to the club only rarely. Without the brown dog it just wasn't much fun.

Furthermore, that ex-husband told me, "It's just like Tho-mas Jefferson said," (he attributed most everything to Thomas

Jefferson), "Any club that would have me as a member and doesn't like my dog can just kiss my ass!"

Burglary and the CIA

MEANWHILE ME AND THAT NEPHEW SETTLED into a new apartment in the Garden District, only a block off St. Charles Avenue. We had lived there long enough to have a couple of parties and enjoy a convenient Mardi Gras when we were burglarized. *And* I'll have you know, I was *at home* at the time. The asshole tied me up with my own telephone cord, threatened me with my very own cutlery, made off with some of my very best stuff, and scared me slap to death. If I hadn't been so scared and blind without my contacts I might have recognized that butcher knife, known it wouldn't cut butter on a hot day and clobbered the son of a bitch. As it was, the dull knife glittered scarily in the moonlight and I was pretty much cowed. And figuring I'd bought the rest of the farm. Well, obviously, I hadn't. After he ran off to terrorize somebody else, I managed to wiggle-

worm my way back to that nephew's suite where there was another telephone. Luck was mine. The scoundrel had overlooked
that phone amongst the truly impressive mess. I summoned the
NOPD. Since I had no idea if they'd come right away or if the
burglar was still around, I then phoned a friend who lived
nearby. My troubles weren't near over with... My friend had
visitors: that ex-husband and the brown dog. They sprang into
the big brown convertible and came racing over, tires squealing.
They roared up right behind three squad cars. My blind terror
was pretty much overshadowed by what ensued.

The dynamic duo leapt from the car. That ex-husband was
screaming at the top of his lungs for the brown dog to "Reconnoiter, boy, reconnoiter!!!" This particular command was not in
the brown dog's repertoire. But, ever alert to the mood swings of
his master, he knew that immediate and decisive action was man-
dated. This was no time for "Lemme just loll around for a few
minutes and aggravate the hell out of this loudmouth." It was
"Placate the lunatic" time. So the brown dog fell to barking and
snarling and slobbering and intimidating the only strangers he
could find: the cops.

Next, that ex-husband started showing the brown dog how
to secure a perimeter. They ran to and fro, back and forth, inside and out, making a great racket. That ex-husband was bellowing all this army-guy, cop-show stuff. The brown dog
launched his blood hound imitation, trying to sniff the nap off
the carpet. The cops were spellbound. When a break in the action allowed it, I said to them, "These would be my ex-husband

and my ex-dog." This information garnered me more of their sympathy than had my recent victimhood.

Much, much later, after the paperwork, that ex-husband and the brown dog took me out for something to calm my nerves. Over a brace of bourbons, that ex-husband leans in and says, conspiratorially, "You know, those cops were most likely wishing I was a permanent member of their team." At that moment I came real close to violating a rule I set for myself in dealing with that ex-husband: we won't talk about his war record. I mean, just right behind my teeth was, "Yeah, they could really use somebody with your military experience."

You see, over the years, he had woven quite a fancy web of war stories. This brilliantly colored tapestry had been unfurled for a number of our mutual friends and some family and untold throngs of strangers in bars around the world. But not for me. He always instructed folks in general and that nephew in particular not to mention this stuff to me because, "You know what a worrier she is."

It seems that the CIA, or "the boys at Langley," would jet him back and forth between New Orleans and Laos, Cambodia, Thailand, and both Nams—in order to carry out "Special missions, mostly on weekends, you know. I was a one-man show and I still can't speak of it." But others would. Like that nephew of his and that lawyer of his (mine too), Charlie Nelson. These two had quite a bit to say about that X's spylife. Interestingly, he was very critical of the modern British intelligence service. He approved of the old MI-5 from World War I, but those new guys had let him down more than once. To say nothing of their onerous, ongoing turf wars.

When I heard about all this, it was all I could do to keep from mirth screeching. This, of course, was precisely the reaction that X least cared to inspire. For their part, the nephew and Nelson managed to keep straight faces through this foolery because for all they knew, it could have actually, by some big old stretch, happened. But, I was there. Every damn weekend. I know where I was and where he was—or the general area anyway—and it sure as hell was not Cambodia.

This is not to say that sneaky maneuvers weren't employed. It was his lifelong avocation to engage in sorties with the local constabulary. He and several of his childhood friends had begun running afoul of the law during their teen years. They grew up in a politically and economically privileged neighborhood with its own police force. These boys were pretty tame by today's standards—mostly they just got naked in public or refused to get out of the vehicle when ordered to. They would stay in the car til the officer came up to the window whereupon they would roll it down just a crack and whisper "Asshole." No AK-47 assaults like kids do now, but it netted a whole bunch of arrests. Enough so that most of the crew were officially deemed "morally unfit for military service." That ex-husband, however, did not have quite enough points to make the category. He missed the Vietnam experience because he was married to me, which even he concedes was a whole lot more fun than rice paddy camping. So, technically, if he'd really wanted to, there was nothing preventing him from signing up anytime he felt particularly warlike, or anytime he felt like following orders or anytime he felt like keeping a neat room. I never ever saw him demonstrate any interest whatsoever in taking orders or neatness, but he was fond of getting in fights. He liked goading and taunting real well too, and would settle for that in a pinch. He was a first rate goader, hard to resist.

One time this guy, Tabby—a wizard when it came to refrigerators and freezers and air conditioners—had been at work all day in mid-summer installing a new central air system at the F&M Patio. And all day he had been putting up with the endless suggestions of that X. It was hot, infuriating work. They kept at it until way after dark. Finally, the filthy, exhausted pair got in the big brown convertible so that Tabby could be given a ride home. They hadn't gone more than a few blocks when the tensions of the day erupted and they began flailing away at each other right there in the front seat. That ex-husband stopped the car in the middle of the street and said, "Let's get out where I can beat your ass." They had consumed several quitting time beers which had given them their second wind. They hopped out of the car and fell to, holding up their dukes and circling one another. Directly, they became aware of their surroundings: a dilapidated neighborhood chock full of thugs and footpads who were gathering to watch and who knows what else. The two men instantly put aside their grievances and were fast friends again. They scurried back in the car and away they went before they both became easy prey.

Staying too Long at the Fair

AFTER NO FANFARE, except from the shockingly energetic Mississippi marketeers, the 1984 World's Fair opened to a mostly local crowd. And it stayed that way, a closely guarded secret. Among the familiar fair faces were mine and the brown dog's. That ex-husband had thoughtfully provided me with a permanent pass. Getting one for the brown dog called for some effort. His application as a music impresario didn't get far due to the photo requirement. Even the most incompetent bureaucrat is often able to tell the difference between a brown dog and a really ugly guy. So the pair went on down in person to press the application for the brown dog's permanent pass. That ex-husband declared himself hard-of-hearing and sorely in need of the brown dog to alert him to certain vicissitudes of life. Says he: "Like if I don't hear a car coming, this brown dog barks to let me know to jump out the way."

Those Fair people could see how this worked and issued the pass. It was several years later that I had the pleasure of telling that ex-husband that there actually is a hearing-ear-dog program. He said that had he known he would've used Plan B: The Blood Sugar Dog—lets him know when his hypoglycemia is acting up. Or Plan C: The Blue Star Dog—warns of ringworm, tettor, athlete's foot & jock itch.

The brown dog spent many evenings happily lurking and skulking among the Fair crowds. He needn't have, since he was legit. He could have marched boldly about; he's just always been a natural born skulker.

Whenever I'd stop in at the Lookout Bar, he'd bound out of the crowd, springing like a gazelle—*boing, boing, boing*— from the floor to the middle of my back. It could knock you down if you weren't ready. The Fair cops would be all over me demanding to know if I were the owner of "that animal."

"No," I'd say stoutly, "He's not mine—he just knows me!"

"Well, okay then," they'd mutter, wandering off with their positions of authority intact.

Sometimes the brown dog liked to really lose himself in a crowd. One time, in the early morning hours that ex-husband came upon a pack of wild dogs. There were about a dozen of them hanging together up the middle of Napoleon Avenue near Tipitina's looking for trouble and bitches. They were loitering around the bust of Professor Longhair, giving one another the big sniffover. They probably weren't really wild dogs, just horny, naughty dogs who had just happened to hook up together. That ex-husband hollered at the bunch to get on away from there. They did take off running, but the sound of his voice prompted further reaction from the group's center: a lone, brown head popped up above the rest. That ex-husband's eyes bugged out as he saw it was *the* brown dog! The man bellowed for the dog, "Come get in this car right now!"

The brown dog looked straight into his eyes and folded his ears back in this weasely way he has, as if to say, "Nuh uh, I'm having fun and I ain't comin' with you." Then he melted back down into the mass of furry bodies and they ran on off like one great big old smelly dog.

The brown dog would never refuse my company so we'd find our spots at the bar for a friendly interlude at the World's Fair. Actually, I would claim my spot at the bar and the brown dog would take his on the bar. Most of the time the crowd was made up of local folks who appreciated the long-standing New Orleans tradition of dogs in bars.

It wasn't long before the Fair Director named him the Official World's Fair Dog. And it wasn't long after that that he was real sorry he had. That ex-husband and the brown dog took to joining the synchronized swimmers. This pair was synchronized in that both were yet again displaying their favorite bathing outfits: buff. They would put on special after hours exhibitions from the diving platform to what they swore was the delight of on-lookers.

In the midst of all this merriment, there was an empty space. One that ought to have been taken up by one of our main deals in life—that ex-husband's nephew, of whom I'd grown exceedingly fond. He was off at Catholic University in D.C. having his own big time, mind you, but I thought he really ought to attend this Fair. I went immediately to that X's other place, the F&M Patio. As was his custom, he was engaged in telling big ole lies to an assortment of miscreants. Folks around there very much enjoyed being lied to, or verbally abused if that's all they could get.

I began to chat up that ex-husband about how we were all having big fun at the Fair while "that nephew of yours is slaving away at school. And I was really missing him and aren't you missing him too?" Before you know it I was sniveling away. I was never one to bandy a snivel about carelessly, so my snivel success rate was quite high.

By the weekend, the Fair had another happy frolicker. All that nephew's little friends were there: Marcos and Scott and Tim and Logan. That nephew had commandeered a piano in The Lookout and the friends had the dance floor. When I saw that the sun was up, I left my group of old people and went to the dance floor to make the young'uns take me home. Some had shed part of their clothing (a recurring theme) and were cavorting in their boxers and jockies. By the by, my own preference in manly undergarments would be the boxer. Men's panties expose that high thigh part where the tan fades to fish belly. Not an attractive look.

"Find them pants!" I hollered. "I want to go home!" The boys responded with a rousing rock 'n roll chorus of "*Find them pants! Find them pants!*" I danced a conciliatory jig, which resembled very much my favorite folk dance of all time: The Dog. (What else?) I herded the happy group, along with the brown dog, into a cab.

The brown dog was as familiar with this procedure as any of us—he would often hop a cab whenever he got tired, bored or just ready to go before that ex-husband. I can assure you that the whole damn world would be ready to go before that X. He never wanted anything to be over with. This was one of the main bones of contention between us because I am famous for knowing the exact time that stuff is over. That would be, of course, the instant that I am ready to go and I need to act on this readiness immediately or I go insane. Which I went on a regular basis with that X because he would never agree that I should leave without him. False imprisonment makes me mean.

But I couldn't seem to act mean enough so that he'd be willing to part with my fascinating self, so I took a page from the brown dog's book and took to skulking off when that X's back was turned. Then that evolved to me telling him, "I'll be right back," after which I'd run like hell. We did reach a kind of tacit understanding that we'd go places together but we just might come home apart. A long time after we split up, we showed up at this same party. After a while, some of my group noticed my absence so they asked that X if he'd seen me. "What did she say when you saw her last?" he queried. They responded, "She said she'd be right back!" He grinned at them, "Oh, she ain't coming back. Not here. Not tonight." He was correct.

Not long after that nephew of his had gotten his fill of our World's Fair and returned to college, the brown dog went MISSING. That ex-husband was distraught over the loss of his companion. Many others were also. Especially me. The brown dog was very popular among those of us that he had never bitten. He had developed an unfortunate taste for humans. What it really was was he'd become addicted to the excitement. He was a hoorah junkie. The brown dog really liked the feel of chomping down on a folk and the squeals that came after. And the clamor. My baby sister Jill was a biter herownself. She thoroughly enjoyed clamping down on some hard to reach spot, like say, the middle of somebody's back. That way they could not beat her about the head and body. Actually, she never did totally give that up.

That ex-husband printed up thousands of flyers bearing a really cute picture of that nephew at age four and the caption: CHILD GRIEVES FOR MISSING BROWN DOG—BIG REWARD! ...and *my* phone number. I got hundreds of calls at all hours. One guy wouldn't quit til I agreed to view his candidate for the reward. "This is not the right dog," I stated repeatedly. He insisted, "But, lady, *he's brown!*"

After several anguished days, one of the bartenders at the F&M gazed vacantly out the window and mused "Is that reward still out for the brown dog, 'cause he's sitting across the street."

There he stayed until that ex-husband lost the battle of wills and went over to fetch him. The brown dog was exhausted and filthy and grinning like a fool. He'd not given a thought for that ex-husband for four fun-filled nights. I gleefully told that X, "NOW YOU KNOW HOW IT FEELS!"

Causes Celebré

NOT MANY THINGS BROUGHT AS MUCH JOY as the safe return of the brown dog. As you know, around here we will celebrate anything, but something good happening is all the better.

We need three things in order to invite folks to help us celebrate: 1) The Excuse 2) The Booze 3) The Food.

Thinking up a reason to have a "do" might take five minutes. The Booze and The Food take longer. (Anyone who's not interested in cooking or eating or drinking—certainly no one I know—can go on and skip ahead to my next chapter.)

As a new Grass Widow, I needed to do some entertaining. Whether I felt like it or not. I knew very well that, left to their own devices, the couples me and that X had for friends were bound to keep him over me. Not that they sided with him—au contraire—it was just the reality that most married hostesses loved having stray guys at their parties. They thought stray women were not only useless, but might turn out to be a dangerous diversion for the odd raggedy-ass ole husband. And some of these women threw tons of parties. All the better to assemble the stray guys, my dear. To what end this assembling? I did not know or care. I knew that the hosts had no say in any of this. If they wanted to do any assembling, well, they had to do it on their own. And so they did. So, I was told. But we're all very glad that things have changed and women no longer devalue other women or themselves either one.

I wanted to at least be kept on those "invite everybody and his dog" party lists. As soon as I could, I had a big party where I myself invited everybody and his dog—which meant even that ex-husband and the brown dog. This showed everybody that we could be in the same room without getting in a fist fight. That X was so taken with the notion that I'd invite him to my first "Do" that he furnished the booze! Wasn't that nice?

I always like to celebrate my own personal birthday—for the entire month. In my case, that would be August, which is the best month except for it being too damn hot. Therefore, at some point, I started celebrating the entire month of October, as well—"Please come to the My Own Birth Month Is Too Damn Hot Party."

Booze is real easy too. Especially easy if supplied by that X. In any event, the only requirement is *you must not run out!* Just go on and lay in plenty, the stuff won't rot, you know. If you overbuy, well then, you're just that far ahead on your next gathering. If you have a bit of a problem with money, and who doesn't, that's no hurdle. It takes a substantial investment to stock a full bar, but not so very much to serve beer and wine. Even less to serve some kind of punch or white sangria. I like **Margarita Punch** very much. It goes like this here:

> *2 12-oz. cans frozen limeade*
> *1 ¹/₂ cups Triple Sec*
> *1 quart water*
> *1 ¹/₂ cups Tequila*

> *Mix these items together the day of your deal. Chill.*

> *Right before they come, add 1 2-Liter bottle of Diet 7-up (save those calories!) which has also been chilled. Serve over ice, in margarita glasses or big wine glasses with wedge of lime on the rim and a straw with a monkey on it. Stir before pouring, the tequila sinks.*

> *This punch is not strong, but tastes great, so you can have a lot. It makes about 5 quarts. If you make too much, you won't have wasted much liquor.*

Pick your Mexican favorites to serve with it. I really like that layered dip that everybody serves. You know the one. Big platter with the bean dip, the shredded cheese, the chopped tomatoes, the lettuce, the avocado. However, I use a layer that most people don't. I apply a final layer made up of 1 cup sour cream, ¹/₂ cup mayo, 1 pkg. taco seasoning mix. It really makes it better.

White Wine Sangria gives you a chance to make use of *really* cheap wine—like the $3 a bottle kind.

> *First make some simple syrup:*

¹/₂ cup sugar
¹/₄ cup water
I tsp. cinnamon

Stir over medium heat til completely dissolved plus 30 seconds more. Cool completely.

In a pitcher, put sliced lemon and orange. Pour in your crap white. Chill. Add the cooled simple syrup.

At party time, add chilled bottle of club soda and serve over ice. You can serve this with other stuff besides Mexican.

To honor the Fall Season (for us, that would be that crispy week in October, or maybe November—we just have to wait and see), I like to have people over for jambalaya. It's a good Halloween Party dish too. Or Mardi Gras, if it falls early when it's still cool. This is a dish that you can have the company help make if you want. I don't ever do that. I prefer to get as much as I can done before hand and make out like I'm a guest. I do most of this prep ahead and the last 40 minutes or so only requires a bit of attention. Even if you bring in professional, hired help, which I do for only about one "Do" a year, some things cannot be deputized. Jambalaya cooking time is one of them. That nephew tried that once when he was making it for his friends in Cozumel. He had them all running to and fro rounding up equipment and ingredients, so it was quite the production. Then he lost his mind for a few minutes and let this old boy from New Orleans mind the pot. The rice came out raw—crunchy. It was

very embarrassing and that nephew was mad as anyone's ever
seen him. By the way, that nephew is famous for his
Jambalaya. It's different from mine. Every cook does their
own deal. You will too.

*Find a heavy pot, like a black iron one maybe. I use either mag-
nalite or my gumbo pot because I don't have a black iron one
big enough which is about 10 quarts. A regular thin pot or pan
WILL NOT DO. It will burn up. If you want to, you can start out
by cutting the following recipe in half (timing stays the same)
to see if you like it before you invest in acquiring a big ole pot.
You can put in just about any kind of meat or chicken. Leftovers, even.*

> 2 Tbsp. olive oil
> 1 1/2 lbs. lean ham chopped
> 1 1/2 lbs. smoked sausage (I prefer HOT) in 1/4" slices
> 3 large onions, chopped
> 2 bell peppers, chopped
> 4 ribs celery, chopped
> 1 bunch of green onions, chopped fine
> 1 large can whole tomatoes or 5 large fresh tomatoes,
>   chopped
> 6 cups chicken broth
> 3 cloves garlic, chopped
> 4 bay leaves
> 1 tsp. chili powder
> 1/2 tsp. each of thyme, clove, allspice, salt, black pepper,
>   cayenne pepper to taste. I like it hot.
> 4 cups raw long grain rice (If you can get your hands on
>   some Louisiana popcorn rice, you will be pretty glad you
>   did. When it's cooking, it smells just like popcorn and
>   tastes real nutty. Don't use minute rice.)

*Brown the sausage in the oil. Add the ham and stir for couple of
minutes. Add the regular onions, bell peppers, celery and garlic
and sauté until tender. Add tomatoes and cook for about 3 or 4
minutes. Add the broth, bring to boil, simmer for 30 minutes.*

Add all the herbs and spices. Add the raw rice. Stir. Bring to boil for 3 minutes, then turn fire very low, cover the pot. After 15 minutes, stir the pot. Recover and cook 15 minutes more. Stir in the green onions. Recover and cook 5 more minutes. Remove from heat and let sit for 5 minutes, fluff and serve.

I did not spell out the above cooking times just for my health. I really mean it; the outcome depends on the timing. And if you lose track and go digging around in there a lot, your rice will turn out gummy. This is not as bad as having it come out raw and crunchy. People will still eat gummy jambalaya. And in some parts of the country where they customarily serve plain rice boiled to a gummy clump, no one will even notice. So, fine. I like to serve salad and bread with the jambalaya—cools off your mouth.

The following sweet dressing over simple mixed greens goes great with the spicy hot. You can add tomatoes, hearts of palm, artichoke hearts, blah, blah, blah. But you sure don't have to. We call this **Cajun French Dressing**:

$^1/_2$ cup (or less) sugar
$^1/_2$ cup canola oil
$^1/_2$ cup catsup (I use Heinz)
$^1/_4$ cup white vinegar (I have used tarragon)
1 tsp. minced onion salt and minced garlic to taste

Me and that ex-husband used to go to this party every year where they had that same menu. However, they did not put out any silverware. You had to use the bread as a scoop and when they ran short of bread, you ate with your hands. They ate with their hands; I didn't. Then some people threw food at one another. Not all of the party took place out in the yard. So some food got tossed about in their living room. And there were those folksingers in the kitchen. The host couple divorced.

This next one is real easy, but pretty impressive. Or messy, I forget which. Maybe both. It's **Bar-b-cued Shrimp!** And it tastes just like the world famous restaurant version used to taste til they kept jacking around with it and cutting corners til it's not even much good anymore. But this is.

2 sticks butter
1 cup olive oil
2 tsp. minced garlic
4 whole bay leaves, crushed
2 tsp. crushed dried rosemary
$\frac{1}{2}$ tsp. dried basil
$\frac{1}{2}$ tsp. dried oregano
$\frac{1}{2}$ tsp. salt
$\frac{1}{2}$ tsp. cayenne
1 Tbsp. paprika
1 Tbsp. ground black pepper
1 tsp. fresh lemon juice
2 lbs. raw shrimp (remove heads, but don't peel)

Preheat oven to 450 degrees. In heavy pan, melt butter, add oil, mix. Add everything but the shrimp. Cook over medium heat, stirring constantly until sauce boils. Simmer 7 minutes, stirring frequently. Remove from heat and let stand for 30 minutes at room temperature. Add shrimp, mix, put back on burner and cook 7 minutes over medium heat til shrimp turns pink. Put in pan (I like Pyrex) and into oven and bake for 10 minutes.

I put that tacky looking dish on a trivet or hot pad right on the table and everyone (me and maybe 3 other people for this amount of shrimp) dig right in. Warm Italian bread goes good.

People like to dip the bread into that shrimp sauce, so have more bread on hand than you normally would. This is the best part. A thoughtful touch would be to have warm, moist wash cloths rolled up to pass around when done. Then everybody doesn't tear off to wash their hands at the same time. It'd also be nice to tell your friends to wear short sleeves.

I love to dine alfresco outside on the deck. Sometimes I'll even cook on the gas grill out there. Or get somebody else to. For chicken, I use the same marinade that the F&M Patio uses.

F&M Patio Marinade:

2 bottles Abita Turbo Dog Beer
12 oz. soy sauce
2 or 3 tsp. powdered ginger
3/4 cup chopped cilantro
3 Tbsp. chopped garlic
2 tsp. cayenne pepper
8 oz. orange juice

I marinate 6 chicken breasts; you want them just covered by the stuff for one or two hours before grilling.

NOTE: If you want to marinate them overnight, then reduce all the herbs and spices by a half, keep the liquids the same. Stick them in the refrigerator. It's great.

Now lemme tell you what I did when I found myself mighty short on cash and time and energy, but long on the desire to entertain. I made **Let's Pretend It's Lasagna.** It looks pretty much like lasagna and tastes great. But real lasagna is ex-

pensive to make—all those cheeses. Here's what you do to come
out with one of those 9 x 15 pans of the stuff.

> *2 big ole jars of your favorite ready-made spaghetti sauce*
> *Cooked ground meat or chopped leftover chicken*
>   *(optional)*
> *I can cream of mushroom soup*
> *2 cans cheddar cheese soup*
> *I lb. lasagna (I use the no boil kind)*
> *Any extra spices you particularly like. I put about one tsp.*
>   *chili powder*

> **Heat oven to 350 degrees. Mix together everything but the la-
> sagna. Do the layering thing. Cover with foil. Bake for I hour.
> Let stand covered for I5 minutes, cut and serve. Do not serve
> this dish to anyone you think might actually be Italian.**

I like to keep the makings for this on hand so I can decide to
have a dinner party at the really last minute. However, if you are
going to serve really cheap red wine you need to open it 8 hours
ahead to let it breath. And chill it too. Try it; you'll be surprised
how much it improves. You can build this lasagna in a throw
away aluminum pan to drop off for the bereaved or the lame too.
Take it over there raw with baking data. It freezes too.

One time at a family Christmas gathering, there was this mix-
up over who was going to be chef. As it turned out it was me,
but I did not know that. So when noon rolled around, I was
happily swigging old anything and water with a twist and having
a genial time. When, lo! Somebody (I think it might have been
Mother) said, casually, "So, when are you going to get around
to putting that turkey on to cook?"

"*Por kay?*" I answered.

"You're doing the turkey, you know," she snapped.

I thought to myself that this was pretty interesting. We were supposed to dine around 4 or 5 o'clock and here it was noon already and the way we always cooked our turkeys was forever. Really. In a real low oven for about 8 or 9 hours.

My solution was to fly into a rage. In my family, we call this

Pissed Off Turkey.

I flipped that oven to 425 degrees. I snatched that big ole blue and white spotted enamel roasting pan out of the cabinet, making lots of satisfying racket. I jerked that turkey bird out of the refrigerator and flung it in the sink. It sounded like a dead body had fallen out of the attic into Mother's stainless steel sink. Thank goodness, somebody had gone ahead and thawed the thing out or we'd have been toast. I washed that baby and removed that crap they stuff up it's butt and down it's neck. I put the salted bird in the roaster, put about $^3/_4$" of water in there too. Put the cover on the 18 to 20 pound critter and got that nephew to put it in the oven for me. Since my mad was wearing off, I wasn't as strong as when I flung the thing in the sink. It was now 12:30.

I cooked it til 4:00 without basting it or even looking at it once. Because who gives a rat's ass at this point. I turned the oven off and left the bird in there for an hour. Then that nephew hacked it up and we ate it.

It was the *best* turkey we ever had. And that's the way I cooked my turkey from then on. However, you can't put dressing up in it or around it. You just have to do that in a separate pan. It's worth it, just for the not having to get all sweaty as you try to baste the damn thing.

What most folks around here do with their leftover turkey is they make turkey andouille gumbo, which is really good. Since they do that, I make **Turkey Tetrazini**. I've gone head to head with other tetra's and mine always wins because of two things: 1) I never use pre-grated cheese. I grate my own sharp cheddar, plus a dab of good parmesan. 2) I add about $^1/_4$ cup of dry vermouth per 8 oz. of pasta. It makes all the difference.

This too, you can put in a throw away pan, don't bake, attach instructions and take to the distressed or stressed-out. And, guess what, it turns out good even if you forget to put in the turkey.

I guess my favorite thing to do is brunch. My favorite things to serve are grillades and grits and champagne. (Say: *gree-ahds* and *gree-uts* and *shay-um-pain.*) I am going to tell you how to do it for four people. It is some trouble. Especially since we're so used to the drive thru. So make lots more and freeze it. Then you'll be ready to have those folks over who can't get along with the first group you invited.

Grillades (for 4)

> *2 lbs. beef round steak, the thinner the better (When I
>   cook this for 25 or 30 people, I get the butcher to slice a
>   10 or 12 pound sirloin tip roast, thin.)*
> *10 Tbsp. bacon drippings (You can go on and eat the
>   bacon.)*
> *2 cup onions, chopped*
> *2 cloves garlic, minced*
> *1 cup chopped tomatoes, fresh or canned*
> *4 Tbsp. flour*

2 ¹/₂ cup beef broth
2 Tbsp. parsley, chopped
¹/₂ tsp. each: thyme, salt, and black pepper
Tabasco to taste.

Pound round steak to ¹/₄" thick. Heat half bacon drippings in big skillet over medium heat. Sauté the meat til brown, about 5 minutes. (Just think how long it takes me to do this part for 30 people! Sometimes I have to get me some help.) Remove the meat to a platter. Lower heat a bit and sauté the onions, green pepper and garlic til lite brown. Stir a lot, then remove to the platter. Stop here and clean the frying pan.

Bump it up to medium heat, add the rest of drippings. Stir in flour and cook until dark brown, stirring constantly. This takes a while, but do it and then you can proudly say that you have made a ROUX! (Say: roo.) If you turn the heat way up and try to cheat it will scorch and be ruint. (Say: rernt.) The good thing is, if you get tired, which you might, you can quit at medium brown. It'll still be good, it just won't look as rich and wonderful—which means a whole lot. So, if you elect to do this, serve by candlelight. Lower heat, slowly add that heated up beef broth, stir well. Add seasonings and meat and veggies. Cover over low heat for 30 minutes. Season if needed. You can add water if you want. Cover and continue cooking til meat is real real tender—spoon tender.

Serve in bowls over grits. It is a little thinner than your ordinary gravy. Make quick grits according to package directions. I use yellow grits. They look better underneath the grillades.

Now I am going to tell you a secret. Tony Chachere's Roux Mix. This is huge. This is pure gold. With this you can make instant roux—just follow directions on package. And it's fat free! Which, I assure you, homemade roux is very, very not. Tony Chachere has made life worth living and I love him.

With the grillades, I like to serve Miss Lexie's Pineapple Casserole (see my sister's book *The Sweet Potato Queens' Book of Love*) or my own **Curried Fruit.** Just FYI, in my experience, women like both of these a lot better than the men do. I don't know why.

> *1 20 oz. can pineapple chunks (save $^1/_2$ of the juice)*
> *$^1/_2$ cup maraschino cherries*
> *1 cup pitted bing cherries*
> *1 big (#303) can fruit cocktail (not tropical)*
> *2 Bananas, kinda firm*
>
> *Sauce:*
> *$^1/_2$ cup brown sugar*
> *3 Tbsp. corn starch*
> *$^3/_4$ tsp. curry powder*
> *$^1/_4$ cup melted butter or oleo*

Heat oven to 350 degrees. Drain the fruit well, reserving $^1/_2$ of pineapple juice. In large bowl, combine sugar, cornstarch and curry powder. Add melted butter, mix. Add all the drained fruit, mix. When you are ready to bake it, add the bananas (thickly sliced) and mix. Pour into buttered casserole. Pour the pineapple juice over it. Bake 45 minutes. This can be served hot or even room temperature.

I make all this brunch stuff up ahead and put it out on warming trays and let folks fend. Have plenty of champagne. If you do not have any champagne glasses, serve white wine instead. It's not worth doing the bubbly without the glass. But either way, it looks mighty festive if you put a whole fresh ripe strawberry in each glass. Take those leaves off.

Here's something. You might already know this, but I just found it out. An alert food package reader told me about it. This is not to be confused with the regular alert readers who belong to Dave Barry. Check out the back of the Domino Confectioners Sugar Box and man alive. I couldn't believe it. I tried it and it's true. It's **Homemade Fudge** you don't have to do that soft balling, candy-thermometering to!! It works and it's fabulous. In case they change the box:

> I lb. Domino's Confectioners Sugar (whole box)
> 6 Tbsp. butter or margarine
> $^1/_2$ cup cocoa
> $^1/_4$ cup milk
> I Tbsp. vanilla
> $^1/_4$ tsp. salt
> I cup chopped pecans

> *In medium saucepan, heat sugar, butter, cocoa, milk, vanilla and salt over low heat, stir til smooth. (This does not take a minute.) Stir in nuts. Spread mixture quickly on buttered cookie sheet. Cool, cut in squares. Makes as many as you cut. Hot damn.*

That is sure enuf fudge in about 5 minutes. Lord, I hope you're not sorry I told you. But you might be like me, I never checked those directions on the box, I just assumed it was that long involved kinda fudge that's too hard when you can just go to the store and buy a Butterfinger.

Post Divorce Sex

Y OU GOT YOUR PREMARITAL SEX, you got your marital sex, you got your extra-marital sex... and, finally, you got your post-divorce sex. It's more common and way, way more popular than you'd think. Well, I don't mind admitting I did it and I did a good bit of it. It began not long after our split-up. Me and that ex-husband went for dinner at Clancy's to discuss something or other like proper divorced people do—if they're not still trying to kill each other. Our meeting was probably over something financial. Or something to do with that nephew, whom I had long thought of as a son-once-removed. From our table on the windowside of the restaurant we could maintain eye contact with the brown dog. He was at his post, guarding the big, brown convertible. In due time we were served our filets, two for me and that ex-husband. The third was for the brown dog, who had his without the stilton but with the demi-glace. He had never much favored the bleu cheeses. Loved a bit of nice aged cheddar, though. Our fellow diners were spellbound at the sight of the tuxedo-clad waiter, at curbside, methodically cutting up the brown dog's meat. They did not turn their attention back to their own vittles until the brown dog's pink tongue had cleaned the platter of the last of the rich, dark sauce and his waiter had cleared. There were a couple of comments, grumblings about "preferential treatment." Frankly, preferential is the only kind of treatment worth a damn and Clancy's is a good place to get it.

For example, they always remembered to bring our afterdinners in small brandy snifters. We hated those liqueur glasses; you always end up with sticky hands. We were enjoying some Kahlua when that ex-husband asked me, "Remember our first date?"

I snorted because, not only did I remember very well, this happened to be the opening line of one of my most favorite rock 'n roll tunes. It was by Ben E. King and we'd would always make our friend Geo Vulevich play it for us on the piano at parties.

"What are you laughing at?" he growled. "Yeah, you were crazy about me right from the start."

This sounded like some more song lyrics and it was making me laugh even harder. You know what's also fun and easier is speaking in newspaper headlines.

I pulled myself together to assert, "I was not! You were the one who was crazy about me. I thought you were a squirrel and I only went out with you because I was embarrassed to tell you that I couldn't get any other girl to go out with you."

"Well, whichever," he muttered. "We did have a good time that night."

This was true.

That first evening had started well. He came to get me with another couple—in their car—one that was better than his awful, raggedy-ass Buick whose floor you could see the road through. I felt safe and relaxed because we had chaperones. So we talked and talked and laughed and laughed and I found out that, expulsions from schools notwithstanding, he was really very bright. Not as bright as me, but bright all the same. I liked it that he wanted to go out with me after learning that I was a smart chick. I couldn't hide my cleverness because we had classes together. I wasn't so bound by the rules of the day (back when possums ruled the earth) that I would actually sacrifice grades to look cute and stupid. But barring that, I did my fair share of looking stupid. And not by design. I could have hung around intersections with my sign that said WILL ACT STOOPID FOR DATES. I would not have been alone.

Covering up my I.Q., as well as my mean streak was tiresome work. At the time, in sex education, I was operating at about the sixth-grade level. I didn't know a thing in the world about blowjobs. If I had, it would have saved me a whole lot of trouble.

After college, when I spent time in the real world, particularly the turning the wheels of commerce part, I noticed that a lot of men not only acted stupid, but they got paid for it. They made it look so fun, I couldn't wait until we womenfolk got our equality and then me and my friends would get to act stupid and get paid for it. I confess that I never got a chance. I think this happens often: when the underdog group gets close to the cool stuff that the upperdogs have long enjoyed, then the cool stuff gets cancelled. Or, more likely, they deny it ever existed in the first place. As soon as we get enough of us in place up top, we can reintroduce acting stupid and getting paid for it. In business there's only about a half a dozen things anyway. The men have just been recycling them over and over forever. Pretending they are brand new and that they just thought them up. When they do think up something new it turns out to be New Coke.

I have also observed that there is absolutely nothing and no one to stop us girls from acting stupid and *not* getting paid for it. Me and all the women I know have done plenty of this. And continue to every chance we get. We just cannot resist. Like my friend Myrtis who was married to this guy for 15 years. She spent the entire time propping his ass up. Trying to make him work and pay his bills, which he would not do a lick of on his own. Working two jobs herownself to pay those bills. Myrtis finally got enough of this and left him—taking nothing with her. Nothing, not even one of their cars. Yep, she flounced outta there, snapping, "I don't want a thing from that man!" That is the epitome of acting-stupid-and-not-getting-paid-for-it.

I was so involved in our first date banter that I didn't notice we had driven out in the country until the car's engine stopped.

The couple in the front seat immediately fell upon one another, open-mouthed. Slurp, slurp. Of course, I couldn't help thinking about what my Daddy would always say whenever a love scene came on TV, "That looks to me like a hog eating a cabbage!" He would say this same thing each and every time. And to this day I can't see two people kiss without thinking about it. Thank the Lord this intrusive thought does not come to mind when I am being kissed. Unless the guy kisses like a hog eating a cabbage.

My Daddy was fond of the repetitive in his sayings. He was a man you could count on. Like whenever I would come into the room, he'd say, "Whither away?" Which I knew, even as a little biddy girl, meant "What are you up to?" And when he'd return from a trip, me and my sister would fall upon him, screeching, "Whadja bring me??!!" He'd fling a forearm across his eyes and holler back, "Hold Off!! Unhand me, graybeard loon!!" We would giggle and laugh and tear into the presents he never failed to produce. And he was very wiley. For instance, there was no censorship in our house. We could read anything we were able. Since there are always items parents don't want their children looking at, he became a genius at instilling self-limitation. He would imitate for us the kind of person who would be reading or looking at this or that trashy thing and, believe me, you would not want to be such a person.

When our first date chaperones disappeared from view down on the front seat of the car, I turned to my erstwhile companion, about to say, "Let's get out of here." I didn't get to say it because he carefully took my face in his hands and leaned in and kissed me. It was brief because we both pulled back from the actual jolt of electricity that passed between us. And it wasn't static electricity either. We stared at each other in surprise and confusion.

This was an unexpected development. "Let's try that again, shall we?" he muttered.

"Yes, let's."

And so we did. Again and again and again and so on, until we were speechless and could hardly catch our breath.

"You know," he said as he swirled his drink and gazed thoughtfully up at the framed caricatures on Clancy's walls, "You surprised me that first time we went out," he said.

"I did? Well, why was that?"

"I thought you were nothing but a stuck-up twit. Oh, I knew you were smart from class and all. But I had been watching you prancing around, giving guys a hard time. You turned out to be really nice and fun. And I really wasn't ready for that kiss."

"What do you mean you weren't ready. You're the one who did it," I retorted.

"I don't mean that. I wasn't expecting that zing," he said.

"Yeah," I agreed. "We sure had something, right from the start."

We drank the last of our Kahluas and wandered out to the car. We found the brown dog well into a nap. So we headed over to their apartment for a nightcap and, I suspected, something more. All that reminiscing had been kind of inspiring.

We hadn't been there too long when I started in with the leave-taking. But nothing would do but that first we watch the Smurfs on television. That X vowed that he rarely missed the program. Ever the gracious guest, I agreed. Directly, we were tussling and panting there on the sofa. And first thing you know, we're up in the bed—our *ex-bed*, by the way. I took his side of the bed, figuring it would be the side least traveled. Well, we followed our tan lines and one line led to another... A very nice time was had by all, including the brown dog who prefers people watching over TV anytime, even the Smurfs. Incidentally, forever after, me and that ex-husband referred to the evening's activities, the finale part anyway, as "Smurfing." So it was pretty convenient for one or the other of us to demonstrate, shall we say, a certain inclination, by hollering, "SMURF'S UP!" We could do this in polite company too. Folks just thought we were talking computer.

As we lay there in the bed nattering, that ex-husband allowed as how the brown dog was no slacker in the romance/lust department hisownself. He and a little Shar Pei around the corner were keepin' pretty steady company, despite an eight-foot chain link fence. The brown dog thought nothing of a chain link fence. (No, it's not what you're thinking—he did not conduct his affairs through the fence.) First, he would complete a sight inspection to locate the softest ground on the other side of the fence. There he would climb the fence just like a man would climb a ladder. He'd pause on the top and drop gracefully onto the soft spot. His wrinkledy, little honey was so lonesome that serious courtship would promptly ensue. As you might imagine, her owner did not look favorably upon this alliance. His cup overfloweth when Champion China Doll—"Dolly" to the brown dog—Pei Ping, presented him with three little brown pups. They were all neatly pressed, just like their daddy. I can assure you that Mr. AKC could not have always been so concerned with bloodlines—for I have seen his children.

"I'm so glad that you and your dog are both having such fine times," I teased.

"What are you talking about?" he murmured.

I assured him, "You know, you don't have to deny, deny, deny anymore—since we're not together. We can both do anything we want."

He allowed himself a small smile and then it vanished, "What the hell have you been doing?"

I offered my own little grin in return, followed by a quick kiss and a hearty hi-o silver and outta there.

It was one of those eight or nine fabulous days we get in New Orleans every year and on the way home I felt happy and pleased and kinda trashy. I had, technically speaking, just done a "One-night-stand" and I had slipped out without saying a proper goodbye! I had loved 'im and left 'im. I know it wasn't like a real one-night-stand, but it felt like I had imagined one would. I liked it quite a bit.

That's not to say that I hadn't always enjoyed the standard social life that came from being married to a wildcat with a hot poker up his ass. We had some very fine times, especially after we got our kindred spirit friends—the Higgins. We did just everything with Jim and Jeanne and it always took all day and into the night. We were nothing if not thorough. Whether we were dining at each others' homes or brunching out or going to a football game. We never did just one thing for an outing. It would always be at least a triple threat. Of course, we consumed many, many cocktails because at the time, everyone did and we all did it real well. We got along famously because they were much nicer and easier to get along with than we were. For example, they had a lot of friends, whereas we had hardly any. We were so grateful to have this wonderful couple to hang with. And they liked us best of all. Goodness knows why. Afterall, our friendship got off to a very rocky start.

It was the first of the dozens of political campaigns we'd sign on for. Matt Gregory, faithful University Inn patron, had qualified to run for office. That ex-husband was able to entice scores of workers with kegs of beer. While I was knocking doors—a hideous pastime—that X and his henchman were putting up campaign signs. And taking down campaign signs of the opponents. This was way before this sort of thing came to be called "dirty tricks." This was normal, regular political activity in New Orleans. This and a whole, whole lot more. That X was just somewhat better at it than most.

Jim Higgins and several others were running against Matt Gregory. Higgins had a particular campaign sign of which he was soooo proud. It was "Across the River," on the other side of the Mississippi River Bridge, in Algiers, where he had grown up. It was a giant Higgins sign, about a hundred feet up in a big ole Oak Tree. It had been a real bear, getting that sign up in that tree. So, he really enjoyed seeing that sign whenever he crossed the bridge to campaign over there or to visit relatives and old friends. This one fine Sunday, he and the wife and kiddies were piled up in the station wagon, on the way to see Maw Maw and Paw Paw. Higgins gets ready to admire his beautiful blue and white sign, waaaayyy up in the tree. But, it's not there! Gone, pecan.

We would later learn from his wife Jeanne that this was the low point in Jim's campaign. That empty tree made his face go red and his nose all pointy, like it does when he gets real mad. And there was too much to do to spend time replacing the sign. Not to mention the money to reprint the giant thang.

Time passed. Our friend Matt was eliminated from the competition. But Higgins made the runoff. We had so enjoyed our foray into the politcal that we decided to check out those two still standing and see if we liked one of 'em. The first party we heard about was for Higgins, so we went. We watched him and his wife for a while and thought they looked nice. The round of glad-handing finally brought the pair to our corner. As that X was shaking hands, he beamed, "So, how 'bout that sign of yours up the tree in Algiers?"

Higgins' neck started to redden and I thought, "Now you've done it! There's gonna be a brawl and I'm going to have to run in the high heels." We were alone and the room was packed with nothing but Higgins people.

To our surprise, Higgins threw his head back and roared with enjoyment. And we started being best friends right that minute.

Jeanne was the knick-knack queen and her mission in life was to help me out with my own knick-knack supply, which was far inferior to hers. Jim's stock-in-trade was good cheer. Never in a bad mood and wouldn't let us be in one either. They were not only very fun but made actual contributions to our material and spiritual well-being.

As I arrived home following my quasi-one-night-stand with my my quasi-, semi-husband, the thought occurred to me that since this had been so much fun, maybe I ought to issue the boy a temporary fishing license (hence the very temporary upgrade from X to semi-). And I knew for sure that I had not had nearly enough exposure to things trashy.

Wait a minute, that wasn't true. Thanks to the ex-husband, I had been exposed to great gobs of things trashy. (His nickname among certain people—from Memphis, mostly—was actually "Trashy.") What I really mean is that I have not gotten to do nearly enough trashy stuff.

When I was real young, this ole woman Maggie Dee told me, "Honey chile, when you grow up, you'll be the kind of a woman that men want to marry—not the kind they trifle with." Of course, this is not necessarily a bad thing. Nevertheless, I was crestfallen. I wasn't old enough to understand her meaning, but her tone was like she'd just told me, "Chile, you will never in your whole life ever get to see the ocean." So I was certain that this "trifling" was great stuff that I was going to completely miss out on.

Maggie Dee was more right than wrong. I have spent little time as the triflee. And have had more offers for marriage than for trifling. I tried a time or two to be the trifle-er, but that didn't seem to work any better for me. When you have to phone up a guy to tell him that it appears that he has failed to take note of the fact that you are not speaking to him—well, you just really haven't hit your stride. I'm proud to say that just because I might be the marrying kind, I didn't keep on doing it. Because Maggie Dee never said I was the marrying-well-kind.

Besides, it's my opinion that a lot of guys really enjoy being trifled with. If you love 'em and leave 'em, they're thrilled! The best you can hope for is to cause them some vague uneasiness. This would be a level of concern about equal with misplacing their car keys.

Butting Inn

AT ONE POINT AFTER ME AND THAT EX-HUSBAND had parted official company, it came to my attention that he had lately been leading a life which was even more unhealthy, ill-conceived, degenerate, and so on, than the one he had heretofore led. Finding himself unfamilial, he was like a blind dog in a meat house. He wasn't just skirt-chasing, he'd graduated to skirt-herding. I was told that he found much efficiency in economies of scale. How fortunate for him that likely prospects were always wandering into his night spots. And the clubs were large enough that he could have several plates in the air simultaneously. In addition, he always had one or two that had the honor of doing laundry, errands, and other "sled dog" duties.

Another signifying change was that I was told these tales to begin with. Information that heretofore I'd hardly been able to pull out of anybody was now pouring in. Folks who were usually scared witless to confirm anything about him were suddenly beating down my door to share. And a couple of his lucky contenders even phoned me up! I could not quite believe it. They actually moaned about how much they loved him and how he was breaking their hearts and stuff.

One of them was a little less annoying than the others and I decided not to jack her around. I said to her, "Didn't your mama teach you anything? Step One: Do not call the ex-wife. Step Two: Do not tell him that you *did* call me because I'm going to give you what's probably the only break you're going to get in this deal—I am not going to tell on you. Unless you ever call me again, of course. Then I am going to bury you. Step Three: Do not be hanging around his place of business, waiting for that big chance to go home with him after closing time. Step Four: When he shows up at your house at four o'clock in the morning, do not answer the door. This is what is commonly known as a booty call. Trust me, if there is booty calling going on, you want to be the caller—not the callee.

"Unless you do these things, I absolutely guarantee that your life will not be worth living. But most importantly, let me urge you to seek your fun elsewhere because this here is just not a good deal."

But the best part was that some of the gossip came from the man himself. He who wouldn't have claimed even the reddest of hands was suddenly blabbing away hisownself. That "sled dog" business came right out of his mouth. Then, surprise, surprise, he apologized for the phone call from the "skunkball," as he dubbed her. I had not ratted her out, she did it herself, I knew she would. I asked him, "What would you do if one of those women gave me any kind of trouble?"

"I would have her legs broken," he sang out cheerily. What a sensible man, I thought.

As our chat continued he offered the tidbit that his alcohol consumption was way more than it had been when we'd been together. I paid mind to this because his consumption had always been, shall we say, abundant. Frankly, I felt a modicum of guilt over having never once in life raised a question about the matter. I had raised questions about many things—many, many things over the years. But never that particular issue. I really hadn't seen it as a problem. In my own defense, we all drank a lot back then. As the years wore on, some cut back, some didn't, and some cranked it up a notch or more. It took quite a while for things to shake out where you could tell who was in trouble. But what concerned me the most was that his hair was just awful looking. It was like a real long dutchboy, but not styled or anything. It looked real stupid. That hairdo of his just put the tin hat on it. I could keep silent no longer. I just felt like nothing would do but for me to butt in his business. So, I phoned him up.

I was all nice and smarmy and fluffing him up like I would do sometimes. Then, in a minute, I said, firmly, "Look, I want to make an appointment with you. There's something I need to talk over." I said it this way on purpose because it was perfectly ordinary for one of us to instigate engagements for lunch or dinner, mainly for fun with a bit of business thrown in. Times and dates and places would be agreed upon then and there.

Not this time. Silence. Then, "I'll check my calendar and get back to you," he said hesitantly.

When a few weeks had passed and he hadn't gotten back, I called again. We set a time, two weeks hence, on account of he was soooooo busy. A couple of days later I got a call from that nephew of his, who had been thoroughly grilled as to the why's and wherefore's of the upcoming meeting, "Do you know what she wants? What's on her mind? What does she want to talk about? What'd I do? Is she mad at me?"

That nephew said, "I told him I didn't have the least idea of what you want with him, but that I wouldn't want to be in his shoes. *That* got him going pretty good, pacing back and forth, snorting and smoking like a chimney!"

"Well fine," I proclaimed.

The night before the meeting, that ex-husband phoned me up, "I'm not going to be able to meet with you tomorrow. But we can just talk about whatever it is right now."

"No, we cannot. Let's do it two weeks from today," I said firmly.

"Well, okay, then," he muttered, hoarsely. He was pretty nervous.

This conversation was followed up with more entreaties to that nephew to find out what in the hell I wanted. That X was really getting edgy. A person like him has just tons of no-telling-what that no-telling-who would want to take up with him. The crop of topics I might have chosen from was vast. This was a man who should have been taken to the woodshed—to remain in permanent residence.

Finally, about three months after the initial contact, I actually got him to the table at Clancy's in the corner of the little room. When I arrived I found that he was already fortified with a couple of anticipatory cocktails, so I launched my presentation without preamble, but looking him right square in the eye, "Now look here, you know how much I have always cared about you and how much I still care about you, in spite of where we're at now. You are one of the most important people in the whole world to me."

He liked hearing this. He loved stuff that's about him, but he knew there was a "But" on the way.

"You just always will be important to me," I added. "*But*, I am just so worried about you and how you are living and how you are just not taking care of yourself at all. And if you don't get a grip and make some changes, well, you are just going to die."

He didn't miss a beat. He looked me in the eye, straight on. His gaze never wavered and he said, flatly, "I-don't-care."

"Yeah, well, I do! I need and value your counsel and your support and your friendship and other things too," I grinned at him. "And, I need very much to know that you are in this world with me. I have always planned on my dying first."

He replied, "That is just *so* selfish. That's how you always were just selfish, selfish, selfish."

Which I wasn't. But neither was he, really. I couldn't brag a whole lot on his gift-giving. But it wasn't because he was selfish. It was just his incredibly bad taste. He hadn't been one of those guys who say, "A boat for me, a blender for her." "A watchband for her, a humongous TV for me." "Golf clubs for me, gensu knives for her." If I'd have been a wise wife, I'd have taken care of my own gifts. But, noooo. I wanted to be surprised. And, honey, I often was. Like the time he got me clothing. He went to a discount store. Not because he was stingy, which he definitely wasn't. It just so happened that he knew where this store was and also it wasn't in a mall. I think it's just possible that he never went to a mall in his life.

It was a stunning moment in gift-opening. There before me was an electric blue sweater with wooden buttons at least four inches across. Its ugliness was unbelievable. The other gifts paled in comparison. Their awfulness is not even worth mentioning.

But sometimes he did good. No, he did great. Like the time he got me the sports car. I always loved sports cars. My favorite was the old Jaguar XKE—the one with the really long nose that you practically laid down in to reach the pedals. At the time, we couldn't have afforded the repair bills on a Jag much less the whole car. Not to mention a spare car to actually drive in case you wanted to go somewhere. What that X did was he bought a Fiat Spider from a friend. It had a real sports car silhouette. And

nice tan and wood grain interior. He had it painted British racing green—just like an XKE. He surprised me with it for
Christmas. It was so cute! I adored that car and him for getting it
and making it better. It was one of the very best gifts ever in life.
I drove the thing around with the top down in January rain. I
ended up with pneumonia. He never once tried to horn in on
my car either. He'd always assume that I would be doing the
driving, if we were traveling sporty.

He could be romantic too, on occasion. He liked to bring
me a corsage for special evenings, like he had for college dances.
And perfume. And he'd be up for a tete-a-tete, if it were at the
Napoleon House in the French Quarter. It was the first place
we went when we moved to New Orleans and he'd always pick
to go there if we were going out by ourselves. Toward the back
of the main room, there was a little alcove for the pay phone,
with a tiny table and two chairs. We would sit in the cubby, listening to the opera music they played and blab away. We'd
drink bourbon in the winter and Pimms' Cup in the summer
and not let hardly anybody use the phone.

I came back to the matter at hand and countered, "I certainly was not selfish, selfish, selfish. And I'm still not. And to
prove it, I'll do anything I can to help you. If you'd get yourself
some help, counseling or something, I'd be more than willing to
go with you and tell them what an asshole you are. I just felt like
I was obliged to speak up about this because it has been both-
ering me. I am really really worried about what is going to be-

come of you. I couldn't just sit by and watch you blow yourself up without saying word one."

"Well, now you have. Anything else?"

"Do you think you could get yourself a new hairdo? I can't believe that Annie is letting you go around town looking like that."

"It's not Annie's fault," he admitted. "I haven't been to her shop, or to anybody's in months. I've just been too busy to get my hair cut."

"Oh, yes, I've heard all about how busy you are. Promise me you'll get Annie to fix you up before the week is out?"

"*That* I can do," he agreed. "Anything else?"

"Not at the moment. Is that all you have to say about what I said?"

"Yep."

"Well, *fine.*"

So, we had some oysters with brie and some turtle soup and fresh fish and a couple of Pimms Cups. We sent some bread pudding over to Linda Ellerbe, who, by the by, was dining on fish also, in the main dining room. She had turned down our initial offer of Jaegermeister. We felt bad, but we didn't know she had given up alcohol. "And so it goes."

Pretty soon we finished and went over to the F&M, where the brown dog was awaiting the treats we'd brought. Bradley had scrounged up some filet remnants and put them in a go-box for us to take for the brown dog. The three of us went out on the patio. We watched the brown dog finish his snacks and begin a leisurely lickfest. The bougainvillea and the stars both looked mighty fine. Our ease was broken when that ex-husband's lackey, "The Rapper," came scurrying over to report that the lights were out in the front bar area and he guessed a fuse had blown.

The Rapper was a critter. One of the collection that ex-husband had assembled into a kind of half-assed entourage. Rapper was probably the most deficient one to ever enlist. He was sorely lacking in both mental and physical assets. To hell with assets, he lacked a lot of just the basics. I don't remember whether or not he could read. But I do remember that he had just enough snap to concoct lies. But they were idiotic, pointless, transparent ones. He was assigned minor chores around the F&M, which he never bothered to begin, much less complete. He had these rheumy, pale blue eyes and moved about with a crablike scuttle. He was shifty and sly and altogether hideous. In exchange for these stellar contributions, that ex-husband gave him room and board.

Among the finest in the panoply of characters collected by that ex-husband was "Poker Dice" Billiot, or Dice for short. Dice was a kind of reverse renaissance man. He managed to accomplish absolutely nothing, in a thousand different ways. One time he was hired for this job that involved driving around in a huge van with big doors that opened out, like car doors. He got to take it home at night because nobody knew that he was taking it home at night. The first week, Dice discovered that it was enjoyable to drive on the street car tracks that ran up the middle of

St. Charles Avenue—still do. Not when street cars were coming. In between runs.

One evening, that ex-husband rode along and soon noticed that because the van was so large, if you flung open the side doors they'd bang into the light poles along the tracks. However, the doors were attached to the van with some really well-made, sturdy hinges. So, it took most of the night for them to knock the doors off. It was at that point—after some eight hours of careening up and down the avenue—that Dice moaned that he was going to lose his brand new job and, thereby, the use of this once fine van. Whereupon, that ex-husband was all sympathy and consoled him. "Dice," he said, "you don't need some chicken shit job driving around all day long in a van."

"You are absolutely right!" Dice declared. "But I really do like the van," he mourned.

Dice went back to his customary source of income. You see, he had this "System" for roulette. Several times a year he'd return to his hometown—Meridian, Mississippi. He'd noise it about that he was gearing up for another trip to Las Vegas where he was going to use his system to make the "Big Score." His old cronies could not bear the notion that Dice might actually make the big score and rise above them on the food chain. So they would all ante up, buying shares in the anticipated score. These were not loans. Not in any way, shape or form. After each and every Vegas visit, Dice would slink back into Meridian all downcast and tail-between-his-legs. He'd confess reluctantly that, yet again, he had failed to hit the Big Score. The cronies took much satisfaction that one of their own would firmly remain so. In fact, in between Dice's jaunts to Vegas, they kept their spirits buoyed by much joshing and funning about "That stupid Dice and big silly dreams. And how pitiful it was that he just never learned." Dice never indicated that he minded a bit the brutal criticism he had to endure on those visits home. He always returned to New Orleans with a satisfied smile on his face. One time I asked him, "Where you been, Dice?"

"Meridian Weekend," he answered. "Forty-four hours of f---ing and fighting and four hours of fixing flats!"

So anyhow the Rapper was quick to point out the blown fuse, but hadn't the least notion of what to do about it. Or more likely his dirt dumbness was just a clever cover for bone lazy.

There are still a lot of fuses sold in New Orleans' hardware, convenience and drug stores, even now because we've got a lot of old-timey electrical wiring to match our old-timey architecture. And in the summertime, we might get your brown-outs just like the real cities do. And, for sure, every time it rains good, some electricity will go out. On this night, the F&M blew the last fuse on hand. No more in the bag. And the days were long gone when the utility company would hustle on over with their big bag of fuses and take care of this for you. Up until the middle '70s they actually used to do that—and for free too. How handy.

A clump of us had gathered outside by the fuse box to discuss who would make the run to store for fuses. Meanwhile our attention drifted to the shotgun house across the street. It was all in darkness but for one room aglow from a TV about the same size as the sofa. Through the curtainless window we could see the little family huddled together watching professional wrestling, mouths agape. A couple of times the room brightened even more when the refrigerator was opened to reveal a plentiful supply of cold drinks—Colt 45 and Barq's Creme Soda were passed around. All was well in Whoville. They did not sense that the Grinch lurked nearby.

The giant TV went dark and we could no longer make out the enthralled, shining faces of this batch of sports fans. We could clearly hear their immediate plaintive queries—and the whines that "We're missing the best part!" And next we could clearly hear the squeaky-scrunch of a chain link fence being scaled and the fap, fap, fap of fast running feet on the dark street that ran between the F&M and the little house. Almost simultaneously, that ex-husband appeared right beside me beaming and only a little breathless. "Look what I found," he exclaimed proudly and gleefully. "Fuses!"

"How lucky," I murmured.

With the F&M's electricity restored, we returned to the patio to resume sky gazing and mouth breathing.

That ex-husband did not make a habit of involving himself in the electrical needs of his neighbors. However, that was not the case with a certain hamburger joint out on Jefferson Highway. It was right across the road from a favorite Chinese restaurant that stayed open late. He'd often end up there for a snack and would just as often pull the power at the hamburger place.

They were modern and had circuit breakers and all. He liked to remove the main power thing so that everything would go off. He'd toss it in the grass. The employees liked it because they got an extra long break while the manager combed through the grass for the power thing.

Cabbages and Queens

I ONLY GET TO WEAR MY TIARA once a year. Now that I hardly ever get asked to a Prom, the tiara gets dusted off for my "Miss America Pageant Watching Party." Me and Jill usually do simultaneous pageanting, conferring by phone throughout. My next plan is to be like Lady Diana Cooper, a gorgeous person of English persuasion. She wore her tiara up in the bed because she said she "never got asked anywhere that called for a tiara." She probably would be quick to remind us of points of tiara etiquette which say, among other things, unmarried wimmen aren't allowed to wear them and no one is supposed to wear them in a hotel!

Pageant watching can be very fun. I have a bunch of friends join me for nabs and drinks and criticizing our betters. Pageant contestants used to have flabby thighs and big behinds, but now they are all hardbodies. However, as the bodies have gotten harder, the talents have gotten even more, shall we say, hidden under a bushel. These days the pageant bureaucracy weeds out all the good stuff during the week of preliminaries or at the state level even. You hardly ever get to see any tap-dancing or dramatic readings anymore. And fire-baton twirlers? Well, they are an endangered species. They should be encouraged, nurtured, protected like those folk artisans and musicians are by the National Endowment for the Arts. This is just as much an important part of Americana as fiddling and quilting and basket weaving and dried-up apple doll making, don't you think? And I think it stacks up pretty well against painting portraits of religious figures and festooning them with animal turds.

Anyway, we get together about an hour before the pageant starts. I have a half dozen or so extra tiaras for those without. We don our crowns and start in on the food, which always includes my homemade **Chicken Salad**. It's nothing very special, but everyone likes it a lot. Probably because it is homemade and not as much like mucous as the storebought kind. This is how you do it for six:

> *10 boneless, skinless chicken breast halves (or 8 if you do*
> *not have a brown dog)*
> *6 stalks celery*
> *1 small onion*
> *$^3/_4$ cup oven roasted pecan pieces*
> *$^1/_2$ cup finely chopped fresh parsley*
> *good brand mayonnaise, salt, white pepper to taste*

Put breasts, three stalks celery, half the onion in heavy pot, cover with water. Bring to a boil, reduce heat. Simmer slowly til breasts are tender. Remove breasts and cool. You could reserve the chicken broth and freeze it or something, in case you might ever cook anything that needed it and you could remember that you had that broth in the freezer, which I never do remember.

Chop 8 of the chicken pieces for your salad and two for your brown dog. Put the dog's chopped chicken in the refrigerator. Chop the other three stalks celery and the other 1/2 onion fine. Add the pecans (which you already toasted and cooled) and the parsley. Mix in mayo, salt and white pepper to taste. White pepper makes a big difference over black pepper. Cover and chill. Right before serving see if you need more mayo.

I sprinkle the brown dog's chopped chicken on top of his dry dog food and serve near the TV as he likes to eat with the group. I usually divided this chicken up into two meals for him because although he was crazy about it, boiled chicken gave him some distress in the lower tract. I'm proud to say, that as crazy as he was about chicken and all manner of folk food, he would never start eating until we all sat down and started eating our food. What a polite dog. His favorite dining place is up in my bed with me. This started when one time I had some surgery and got to have my meals served to me in the bed by a housekeeper. She was a very thoughty housekeeper and figured I would enjoy dining en famille, so she fixed a plate for the brown dog too. He was visiting to keep me company and protect me while I was in a weakened state. Well, did he ever take to that. He was just crazy about eating in bed. In fact, after I was all healed up, he'd still sometimes refuse to eat until I had moved his food to the bed. Obviously, this is a pretty satisfying thing to teach someone else's dog. I always liked to send the brown dog back to that ex-husband with something new and different if I could.

Pageants are always entertaining, but some are better than others. The best one I ever saw was the "International Mother/Daughter Pageant" on cable. All the moms wore those industrial strength pantyhose under their swimsuits. Almost all of them had cellulite but it was smoothed out by the hosiery. Sometimes the stockings fit so tight that the contestant could not bend her knees to walk. No talent of any kind was in evidence and some of the mothers and daughters appeared to have just met each other that day. Pageants are chock full of this amusing and diverting stuff, though the competitors are deadly serious. However, I have noticed that even we watchers tend to get kinda serious if "our" candidate gets to the finals. "Our" candidate would, of course, be a girl from Louisiana or Mississippi, since that's where we are all from.

You know how folks remember where they were when something big happened, well, a whole lot of Mississippians remember where they were when Miss Mississippi won Miss America—two years in a row, mind you. Poor old Mississippi didn't have much to be proud of back then, so anything the least bit positive was more than welcome. Some people think it's still like that, but that is just not true. Besides, we are looking good now that some states have started electing professional wrestlers and bodybuilders to public office. And Louisiana always has held up its end in the indicted public officials category. But now that I have dual citizenship, I don't want Louisiana to look foolish either. My "ponder heart" has to belong to Mississippi because six generations of my family stand in silent claim.

Louisiana claims me like she claims so many others—we volunteer for the pure fun of it. And for the bountiful crop of eccentrics that thrives here. Like the "Lady in White" who shows up regularly for mass at one of the big churches on St. Charles Avenue. She wears clothing that used to be white. When it was clean. She never says anything to anyone. Just about the time the Dean takes his position, she marches up the center aisle to a front row seat. She minds her business and does right during the service. At the end, the choir and acolytes and everybody files out. Then the Dean goes and turns and gives the blessing. While he's doing that and a lot of heads are bowed and eyes are closed, she hustles after him. When she gets about halfway down the aisle, she whirls back around, looks up at the stained glass windows behind the altar, flings her arms in the air with white-gloved hands pointing skyward. Touchdown!!

And the woman we call "Jerky Lady." She's spent so many hours hiking St. Charles Avenue that her skinny body's been sun-cured til she looks like beef jerky. Back and forth and back and forth she hikes, with her neck out long and her long, wild hair, dried out and bleached nearly white and blowing back. Not even our humidity can keep her plumped up.

A very well-known character was the late Chicken Man, who is survived by his wife, Chicken Woman. They scratched out a living as conjurors. It was apparent to anybody who looked twice that they did enough business to keep themselves supplied with more than a sufficiency of alcohol and other mood altering products. Folks would commission the Chicken Couple to cast spells to influence fortune and fame and romance and revenge and whatnot. This they would eagerly do, using their favorite spell-casting materials: chicken feet and necks. Hence the name. If a good little while would go by without any customers needing a spell, then the pair would do their volunteer work—in order to maintain a certain minimum level of spiritual energy. That stuff will go rusty on you if you don't use it. This consisted of standing on their front porch, admonishing and exhorting the neighborhood. They also wanted to be sure all their spiritual bases were covered. So they devoted some of their time to Christianity. They were the founders of the Smoking for Jesus Ministry. Their work in the cause consisted of them and a couple of their raggedy-ass friends sitting around smoking cigarettes, or whatever. The puffs would be punctuated by one or the other of them hollering out, "I give this to the GLOW-REE of JEE-SUS!!" And they'd blow the smoke toward heaven.

I wonder if the Chickens were friends with Mr. Allah M. God who wound up in traffic court. Mr. God was fond of exhorting and admonishing also. Which he did to the judge, yelling, "You cannot prosecute God!"

The judge retorted, "Well, I'm going to, today."

When the judge asked him his age, the response was "I am the Alpha and the Omega."

I'm using this the next time somebody asks me my age.

The judge figured he wasn't going to tell his age, so he was booked with public intimidation, disturbing the peace, disorderly conduct, and threatening a public official. That last one was because he bellowed that he'd be back to punish all who participated in hurting God.

I've always been partial to the mini-security-guard that used to stand watch over Audubon Place. This little bitty man in a little bitty cop suit was all that stood between the fanciest enclave in town and the rabble. And he was mostly wore out from horrific weekends spent with his rampaging wife, "Big Mamou." She was not little bitty and she was not a bit happy with anything about her little spouselet. He would come over to the University Inn after his guarding the rich shift was done. Over many beers, he would bemoan his fate—his unfortunate and inescapable attachment to Big Mamou. And how she could read minds. She could always tell when he'd been up to something and the punishments were fierce.

And there's my own friend, Gisela, as terrifying, in her way, as Big Mamou. Her appearance was memorable: skin like tree bark, face like Cruella deVille, hair like Lucille Ball. She was very artistic; she created sculptures out of lint from a clothes dryer. Since she was unable to produce sufficient lint herself, she made the rounds of washaterias and cleaned out their lint traps in exchange for getting to keep all the lint she can harvest. She tried contacting the big commercial laundries, but they refused to part with their lint. They claimed to be engaged in a massive recycling program. However, they wouldn't specify exactly what the lint was recycled into. I wondered what third world country was the beneficiary of the recycled lint and what form might it take.

Gisela's personality was on the controlling side. There was this little public park that she had decided that she was the boss of. Through force of will, hers and a few of her friends, the park came to be known as Dog Park. She was a dog lover and felt that dogs need somewhere in town to run free. So despite ordinances and posted signs to the contrary, Gisela often took her flock to the park and set them loose. One evening the pups went bounding through the middle of this picnic that some dogless types were enjoying. Their blanket got muddied and picnic paraphernalia went flying. The hostess of the picnic also went flying—in Gisela's face—demanding that she leash and restrain the dogs. Gisela refused and a fist fight ensued. The police were called. Who should arrive in response but Officer Bowser! Gisela asked him was he making that up. He was not amused and ran them all off.

This was not the last scuffle that would break out in Dog Park. And later on, Officer Bowser was not so accommodating. The next combatants, and they were women too, had to go to court over it. An uneasy peace between the dogged and the dogless continues to this day.

Gisela also tried to dictate both menus and guest lists, should you get up the nerve to invite her to your house. If she were anywhere else, this would not come up: there would be no invitations. But in New Orleans, she blended right in. It truly was her appearance that set her apart for I know many folks that are just as self-absorbed.

I have always found it curious that a place so steeped in tradition, so clinging to the old-timey notions of tradition would be so lax in the common courtesy department. Just try to get an RSVP. Just try to get a philharmonic audience to be on time, shut up, and quit opening cellophane candy wrappers. Just try to suggest that a pregnant girl's momma might not ought to throw her a baby shower—whether she's married or not. Just try to suggest that you might look greedy if you put your gift list in the envelope with your wedding invitation.

Then there's the "Cemetery Pals." These two real good girlfriends got to be beyond middle age and they'd never married. They decided they probably wouldn't, so they went in together on their funeral arrangements. They spent about a half a million dollars building a marble mausoleum in Lakelawn Cemetery. After it was finished they threw a party in it and invited about 300 friends to come on out to the graveyard and have some champagne and hors d'oeuvres with them. Of course the little death mansion wouldn't hold but about a dozen folks, really crammed up in there. So they rented a couple of little tents, which was a lucky thing. It rained the day of the soiree. Enthusiasm ran high anyway; about 200 showed up. Some brought mausoleum warming gifts.

Best of all was this old guy whose big old house and yard were in such a bad way that his neighbors took up money to try to buy him out. He was all weird and mean and wouldn't sell for anything. This one neighbor videotaped the house to show the health department how awful things really were. He forgot and left the tape running all night. Imagine his surprise when the tape revealed that the old guy was coming in and out all night long, with a 50-pound-bag of dog chow, feeding the rats! Some would eat right out of his hand! A TV crew came in the middle of the night and caught him doing the same thing. He explained that he liked rats just fine.

Yessiree, we in the South love eccentricity but we are all *so* glad to have some other states be the goat for a change.

I was so tickled to see that rich old Massachusetts came up dead last on the IRS list showing charitable contributions by state. Guess who was first? Poor ole Mississippi I'm proud to say. And they were first by percentage of income, by per capita, and by the actual dollars given. Talk about giving til it hurts.

Last year I got to wear my tiara an extra time. My friend Bill invited me to his birthday party and he seemed pretty worked up about the event, so I asked him could I wear my tiara and he said, "Oh, would you? That would be just grand!" So I did and it was. A couple of months after the birthday party, I had occasion to explain to someone about my "Pageant Watching" parties. She asked me, "So how come you make fun of that pageant stuff?"

"Huh?" I countered, while wondering how I could do otherwise. "What do you mean?" I finally managed to squeak out.

"Well, weren't you involved in that sort of thing?" she answered.

"What do you mean—involved?"

"Well, everybody's always known that you used to do that kind of stuff," she retorted. "Your ex-husband told us from the beginning when we first met you how you were Miss Mississippi, and all."

Right about here was where I was struck both dumb and blind. My head was spinning in disbelief. Dozens of thought fragments flashed through my mind: "How could... When did he... Who all did he... How come nobody every said anything?" And, "Oh Lord, I wore that tiara to that birthday party and Bill and all them other people thought it was my real crown from being Miss Mississippi. I guess they thought I was one of those pitiful, desperate-for-attention middle-aged pageant refugees or high school football star, dying to dredge up any excuse at all to mention their moment of glory. And I wish I were dead."

I started cussing and moaning and covering my head with my hands. But then, I looked on the bright side. The reason nobody ever said anything to me was that nobody questioned it. So, I got the credit for having been formerly goodlooking and talented, to boot. And without the embarrassment of having entered such a contest. So, fine! As for Bill and them, well, I'd just phone him right up and explain and force him to pass the word and I'd be good and damn careful where I wore a tiara the next time out of the box. But if anybody ever does come up and ask me I am going to say, "Yes, I was Miss Mississippi and I won entirely on the strength of my fire-baton-twirling."

The End Justifies Nothing at All

T HAT EX-HUSBAND WENT TO NEW YORK to put that nephew of his on a plane bound for Amsterdam. He was treating the nephew to an indefinite Grand Tour. Well, for six months at least.

I was relieved on behalf of the nephew that he got to go alone. I was half expecting that X to tag along at the last minute. And since he was footing the bill it could have taken some tricky maneuvering to leave him behind. That ex-husband loved to go places with that nephew of his because he deluded himself that they were contemporaries, and buddies to boot. That ex-husband fancied himself young-at-heart and so forth and so on. As a matter of fact, he thought of himself as young-in-face-and-body as well. The reality was, of course, somewhat different. Although that ex-husband had the constitution of a teenaged mule, he had crammed a couple of lifetimes into half the space. And it was beginning to show. While still plenty attractive for what he was: an almost middle-aged lunatic with wild blood-shot eyes, Clarabell hair from too much sun, pants with the waist always sitting either too high or too low and way too much furtive mustache-licking. An altogether alarming picture which that nephew was pleased he would not be seeing all over Europe. The prospect of that ex-husband on the French Riviera...

Instead, he returned to New Orleans where a persistent backache landed him in the hospital. It wasn't the kind where somebody says they're "down in their back." It was big pain coming from deep inside him. He would have a whole lot rather been in Norway with that nephew, slapping down $10 a pop for warm beer. It turned out he had pancreatic cancer. I don't think it was possible for the news to be any worse. That ex-husband's father had died of that same thing. And he did real quick—less than six months and no treatment at all that I know of was undertaken. I checked around and what I found out was that everybody died from this disease in six months, no matter what they did or didn't do. I don't know if that ex-husband knew that or not, but he chose to do battle. He had this surgery that was so drastic it rearranged his whole insides. I think it had a five-year survival rate of about 1%—which really meant that nobody survived. He didn't need to know that either. He was already terrified after years of lower level fear. He'd started having physicals before he was thirty years old, but he never talked about why he did that. It wasn't like he led this healthy life or anything.

I was scared to death too. I came home from my job most every day and had to either get in the bed or take a hot bath to get warm. It was the middle of summer. I felt cold and quivery, like I do when I wake up from a nightmare. The marrow of my bones was ice cold mercury and I ached with fear. I felt as scared as if it were happening to me. And shocked—to the core. The strongest man in the world was in mortal danger. He had such personal power. He seemed indestructible. If he could be this vulnerable, where did that leave me? There was no safe place anywhere in the world. I realized that I had always counted on this man to provide that last sanctuary, should I ever need it. Who would hide me now?

During the radical surgery, the tumor had been successfully removed, so that ex-husband had a shot. But he would be required to make some actual contribution toward getting well, i.e. taking nothing by mouth for a good 6 to 8 weeks so his innards could grow back.

Well, I'm here to tell you that the rule has not been made that this critter could not or would not break, bend or ignore. With his very life on the line, that X amused himself by sneaking water and, on less frequent occasions, Listerine. He would go through this elaborate pantomime—like he was gargling and spitting—when he was actually swallowing. As you might imagine, this greatly lengthened his hospital stay. So I visited as much as I could, most every day. Even if it was just to run in and bring him a little something to make him more comfortable or make him smile. One time I brought him my own personal "get cozy" blanket. Because he had trouble getting warm too. It was a white flannel sheet that was worn real thin and real soft from lots of wallowing and hundreds of washings. I didn't have time to run it through the wash, so I just took it on to him like it was. It wasn't nasty or anything. He grinned and said, "This smells just like you. L'Air du Temps." Naturally, he would know my fragrance since it hadn't changed in twenty years. But I got a big ole lump in my throat anyway.

Another time I brought him a giant blow-up of this snapshot of that nephew and two friends. They were all three in cut-offs, tanned and clearly enjoying a day of boating—beers in hand. I'd had it made and framed for that ex-husband for his Christmas present. But it was such a cheery thing to look at. I have the snapshot on my desk and it always makes me smile. I went ahead and brought it to him, even though Christmas was still weeks away. I thought we could hang on the wall across from the foot of his hospital bed. It was an icy stab in the heart even though he was grinning at me when he said, "That's my Christmas present, isn't it? You just don't want it to go to waste!"

I retorted that I would never waste a fine picture like that. I would just give it to some other asshole. "You're not the only asshole in the sea, bucko!"

"I know, but I'm your favorite," he chuckled.

However, a big contribution that I made was bringing pastry treats to the hospital staff every Saturday since I figured they were about ready to smother him with a pillow. If I were taking care of sick people I know I'd get so annoyed with the ones who wouldn't get better. Or even if they just hung around the hospital for a long time. Which he did.

But the best thing of all that I did for that ex-husband was to track down that nephew of his and urge him to cut short the European tour and return to New Orleans. He did and showed up unannounced. That ex-husband was mighty tickled and surprised.

The many hours that nephew spent with that ex-husband were the best medicine for him. I would visit most every Sunday evening too. We three would watch *60 Minutes* as we had on so many Sundays when we'd all lived together. It was unsettling, in a way, to me. Out of time and out of place, but as familiar as Mike Wallace's ole road-mapped face.

The hospitalization dragged on and on and on and on. The first few weeks he was able to walk about the halls, dragging that IV thing along beside him. I would often stroll with him. Then I began to pull the IV for him. Then he couldn't manage a stroll at all. Weeks turned into months. I prayed as hard as I ever have. No longer the perfunctory inclusion of that ex-husband on the tail end of the "Bless so and so's." I was petitioning separately for his healing. I conceded that he did not particularly deserve any more chances. And that nobody knew better than me what an asshole he could be and so often was. But, I asked God, couldn't He let him skate by just this one last time? I am sure I made fancy promises in exchange, but I can't remember what.

I even made the suggestion to God that he could just go on and heal him up. Afterwards, if that X didn't do right or some better anyway, well, then He could just strike the son of a bitch with lightning or a truck.

The brown dog was feeling poorly too. He hadn't laid eyes on that ex-husband since this whole ordeal began and he was crankier than ever. Meanwhile, in between praying for that X to get well, delivering baked goods to anybody wearing white and thinking up clever trinkets to bring in to amuse the patient, I had quit my corporate job at Barq's Root Beer. I had become an entrepreneur. I had purchased for dirt this little café that had already been in business for about fifty years. It was near Tulane Medical School. It catered to med students and physicians and other medical personnel—like I hadn't had just about a bait of medical types—and a smattering of tourists and local eccentrics. It came ready to roll with a dandy bunch of women already on staff.

One day after the lunch rush was over at the café, me and that nephew went on to the hospital for our regular visit. When we got to that ex-husband's room we were told "He's just drawing his last breath, but you can go on in. Watch what you say, he can still hear you." Me and that nephew locked looks: How can they tell that this is the moment?

He didn't look much different to us than he had for days and days. But without a word between us, we two were of a mind. We would take their word for it. So we marched right in the room and took our places, one on each side of his bed. We began patting and stroking and soothing him. And talking to him. We told him that overall he'd done a real good job—he had most certainly fought the good fight (hundreds of good fights as he well knew!) and he could go on and go if he wanted to.

My chin trembling so bad I could hardly speak, I said, "You have done a particularly fine job on that nephew of yours. I know that you have always given me all of the credit for raising him, but really, you were just as much responsible for him turning out so good as I was." Of course, that nephew's heart warmed right up hearing this. And it was the truth. If I could of ordered me up a youngun, I'd of picked one exactly, precisely like that nephew. Part of the reason I found that nephew to be such a wholly satisfactory individual was that, in spite of being raised by us and being kin by blood, he didn't have any of our faults. He had a couple, they just weren't the same as ours. Folks hate their own faults way more in other people than they do in themselves.

"And," I went on telling that ex-husband, "you were a truly generous person. Way, way too generous. Lending money to so many people. And hardly any ever paid you back. You never even asked them to."

"Yeah," added the nephew, "like the Neville Brothers, and Bullet. Except didn't Bullet finally pay his back?"

I said what a good and faithful friend, advisor, protector and provider he had been to me. And that nephew said ditto.

"And, furthermore," I said, "You went way beyond the call

when you took the rap that time for Eddie, claiming you were the one driving and that that bag of weed was yours not his. He probly would have been ruined and you, well..."

I wanted to tell him that he had been the very best in the sack too, because I knew that's what he would really really like to hear more then anything. But, to tell you the truth, this was the closest thing to a supernatural experience that I'd ever had or probably ever would have. And I felt so very proud to be a part of his last moments on the earth—the most important event in his life. More important than coming into this world. It was the most mystical thing I had ever done. It seemed like it would be unseemly to bring sex into it. So me and that nephew just kept on patting him and telling him we loved him and that we'd miss him. It took ten or fifteen minutes for him to finish taking his leave of us and his body which was plumb wore out by now. We were very tired too, me and that nephew. It had been a hard thing to do, saying good bye in that way to someone so close. It was hard, but it was right. How strange that although me and that ex-husband had been apart for years, my voice would be the last thing he heard on this earth.

Afterward, the nursing staff told us that they had never ever seen anybody give their loved one a proper send off before they saw us do it. "Folks most always run away and leave 'em to do it alone," they told us.

I'm telling you, we really felt good that we had instinctively done exactly the right things. Because we sure didn't plan it. We'd never said word one about what we'd do if the time came.

Our only regret was that we hadn't thought to look up towards the ceiling and maybe give a big Adios. You know, because of all those near-deathers who say that you hover around up there for a while.

I also regretted that that ex-husband wouldn't get to see my new business. Or, rather, I wouldn't get to see him see it. Who knows what all dead people can see. Personally, I never could decide if I wish that dead people can see us or not. But if they can, I sure hope they are less critical than they were when I knew them.

Anyway, me and that nephew set about planning that X's funeral. That nephew said, "You know, he always wanted to be cremated." I was thinking that actually it was me who had always wanted to be cremated, but, whatever. It would be at Bultman on St. Charles Avenue and our spiritual advisor, the Reverend Bob Dodwell and his wife Mary, formerly of St. Anna's Episcopal Church on Esplanade Avenue would run the show. Anyone who wanted to would be invited to say something. There would be bag pipes—which at the time I had never seen at an ordinary funeral before, but now everybody's doing it. The late Jim Monahan of Molly's Irish Bar arranged for the piper. Our old friend, Philip Carter helped us put together a real nice obituary for the *Times-Picayune*. Later, there was another nice piece by Clancy DuBos in the *Gambit Weekly* which was picked up statewide.

Obituaries make some of the best reading you can find in New Orleans. The *Times-Picayune* doesn't seem to have any guidelines and the bereaved don't seem to have any self-imposed limitations whatsoever. The death announcements sometimes run on for dozens of paragraphs, enumerating each and every life activity of the deceased, however mundane. There was this one I saw that was chock full of exclamation points and words in all caps: Mr. Jones drove a TRUCK!! He was a long-time member of ALCOHOLICS ANONYMOUS!! He had a LIBRARY CARD AND HE LOVED HIS BACON!!"

And the lady who had made it to 103, whose main source of pride was that she could still wear her LSU cheerleader outfit from 1910. Which, it was stated, she wore to all important gatherings during the last 25 years of her life.

I like the write-ups for the guys where the names of the surviving "wife" and the "companion" are both listed. Or sometimes multiple companions. A whole lot of them include the names of beloved pets—that always makes me snivel.

Some funeral plans are printed in a most straightforward way. Like "In lieu of flowers, please bring cash donations to the church for funeral expenses." Or "Services will begin at 2 PM with the Memorial Throwdown to follow."

I love the "dueling obituaries." This is where the deceased clearly led at least two separate lives. Each family publishes their own obituary, containing all the same data regarding the arrangements, but with different survivors' names. I have not yet seen one where two different services were held. Along with death notices, local newspapers also print thank you notices from the survivors for services and kindnesses rendered. One day I read where the family of Mr. Smith was thanking The Rev. Outshine of the Whatever Church of God and thanks to Mr. & Mrs. Redevelop Pithy and Mrs. Anemia Turner and Mr. Erring and Dusting Brewer for all their help. The very next day, there was another thank you from the family of Mr. Smith. This one was by way of making some corrections. It should have been The Rev. Brown of Woodhaven Church of God. And thanks to Mr. & Mrs. Rudolph Petrie, and Mrs. Anna Mae Turner and Mr. Erwin and Duston Brewer for all their help.

Memorial notices are also popular here. For special holidays, like Mother's and Father's Day, Easter and Christmas, there might be pages and pages of them—for people and animals, living and dead. With photos. I loved the one of Mr. Norman Morales, grinning and giving a great big ole thumbs up! Just any tribute you take a notion to pay, just go head on. Sometimes family and friends of the departed use these memorials as vehicles to settle old scores:

In Loving Memory of my Father, John Doe

As your favorite child, I'd like to say that you were always very forgiving to your other three children and so loving toward your most beloved wife, the late Jane Doe. You may have spent the last 3 years of your life with that second wife, Trixie Doe and her three children, but you always managed to sneak plenty of special time with your real family. I am glad you are at rest with our mother—your true beloved. You always used to say that she was the love of your life and you died on the anniversary of her death to prove it!

Your loving daughter, Sally Doe

So, I guess she told ole Trixie, didn't she? Can you imagine what it would be like to stumble down to breakfast and find that alongside your coffee some morning?

There is a fledgling cottage industry emerging which serves to present the message in poetic fashion. I saw this one poem that said, in iambic pentameter that we know our loved one was murdered, we know who did it and we are gonna get you, sucka. In contrast, another sweetly asserted, "There are no secrets to share or problems to air. We just want to give a shout out to our good friend Pork Chop." That's another source of enjoyment. A lot of the obits include the nicknames of the departed. I've collected them for years.

Women have ones like "Princess," "Pretty," "Pumpkin," "Sugar," "Mumsie," "Bitsie," "Chickie," "Duckie," "Gidget," "Sweetie," "Duchess" and so on. There were two sisters called Heatsease and Caldonia—two more known as Peanut and Brittle. There was a taxidriver known fondly as "Bump the Rider." There were men called "Darlene," "Patsy," "Bimbo," "Dimples," "June," "Holly," and "Lucille's Boy." Come to think of it, way more guys have their nicknames printed.

Some late guys:

Captain
Mr. Fixit
Colonel
General
Duke
Mr. Wizard
Equalizer
Tutty
Dinky
Head
Coke Machine
Tiny
Zip
BooBoo (an oft-used one)
Flip
Egg
Popcorn
Cat Daddy
Squinch
Juggie
Dogboy
Luv You Man
Alley Cat Eyes
Quickie
Penthouse

Delite
Buttercup
Tut Tut
Funkadelic
Doodle
Short Wind
No-Way
Toe-Licka
Woolite
Bangtail
Treasure
Topsy
Bosco
Tea Bell
Buzz
Tank
Bear
Firecracker
Brownie
Blackie
Fuzzy
Flappy
Froggy
Iceman
Pougie
Choose
Tricky

Graveyard
Jesus Hots
BoDillie
Life of the Party
Barefoot Louie
Butterbowl
Squirrel Man
Raddie Mouth
Bo-Legs
Greenapples
Easy
Chickadee
Spud
Tequila
Candyman
Popsicle
The Bookie
Booger
Bugger
Boodie
Doodie
Doozie
Dirt
Devil
Darkie
Beaver
Hippo

Jam
Jelly (but no relation)
Pony
PeeWee
Sitting Bull
Czar
Corn
Buffalo
Irish
Money
Whitey
Prince
Tweetie Bird
Mickey Mouse
Grits
Monkey
G-Daddy
Nookie Nuggie
Putt Putt
Pluto
Red Boy
Red Son
Ringo
Rabbit
Squirt
Stumpy
Moot

Wiggly
Catfish
Bat
Funky
Huggie
Koochie
Moochie
Poochie
Squinchie
Squeeky
Light Bulb
Hacksaw
Joker Mouth
Pluckeye
Fishstick
Slow Dog
Moon

One of our mayors was named Moon. Me and that X campaigned for him. We had this other one named Dutch. We campaigned for him too. Besides being known for his good nickname, Dutch was known for a few other things. One was that he was the first black mayor of New Orleans.

He was the first black guy to do a whole bunch of stuff. Like law school and be a judge and so on. He was also pretty famous for his meanness. I am not speaking ill of the departed, which he has. Everybody knew he was mean. Dutch said so himself and seemed proud of it. One of his favorite things was revenge. I kind of like it myself. However, I've never been in a position to extract much of it.

Dutch also liked to prance around and make out like he was going to qualify to run for some political office or other. Then nobody else would have the nerve to sign up to run for it. It would freeze the action in the political contributions department while everybody stood around waiting on Dutch to decide what he was going to do. The goal was: "Try like hell not to piss Dutch off." He knew very well what folks said behind his back. He just laughed and said it was "creative tension."

He came to this annual Christmas party that me and that ex-husband had. One year, I made this awful looking dip out of eggplant (eggplant cooks up ugly unless you bread and fry it) and tomatoes. It was lurid—as though it had been pre-eaten. But tasted pretty good. Dutch spotted the stuff from two rooms away. He said his momma used to make that and he hadn't had any in years and years and did I have any Tabasco? Which I did. So he used nearly the whole bottle doctoring the eggplant and then ate the whole bowl.

Of course, Dutch had a big ole funeral. He lay in state at Gallier Hall and people stood in line for hours to pay their respects. There were television crews milling about, interviewing folks, getting their notions of Dutch's long career and so on. My favorite was this guy who thought he was in the line for Elvis.

Other cute nicknames I've seen included: Pops, Buddha, Slick, Deuce, Fishbone, Bull, Thunder, Poo, Weasel, The

Shrimp Man, Sheepy, Snake, Red Garter, Pork 'n Bean, Possum, Wheaty Boy, Major, Premium, Rubber Leg, Pusher, Vanilla, Smooth, Rotten, Too Soon, Uncle Pap, Shine, Muskrat Joe, Mullet, Cigar, Goat, Kernal (a misspelling, perhaps?) Country, Low Rider, Nasty, and Killer. The dead guy named Shorty, survived by his wife Madonna.

There was a man called "49" who died at age 81.

All on the same day, I read about WaWa, YaYa, JoJo, MoMo, and BoBo.

I loved the guy named Chicken 3, who's sons were Pecka, Peckie and Chicken, Jr.

Another favorite of mine was the late man who had surviving brothers named Footsie, Nappy and 'Sup.

Don't you have to love Troy Donahue Fontenot?

So far, my favorites are the guy called "Dump-Turtle" and the twins called Fennel and Chervil.

I really wish the newspaper would make it a rule that if you want the nickname printed in the piece, then you will be required to give an explanation of how they got that nickname. Because I would really like to know.

You know, one of the things I whispered to that ex-husband in the hospital was about a nickname. I told him, "When I talk to the *Picayune* about your final arrangements, I am going to make sure to tell them that your nickname was 'Pawn Shop.' He got really still and waited for me to go on. I did. "That way everyone will then get to know what only a few dozen women of dubious character were surprised to discover—that you have three balls." He squeezed my hand and tried to smile at me. And, no, of course, he didn't really have three balls and that wasn't his nickname. I just always did like to tell him stuff he wasn't expecting. He liked it a lot, too.

That ex-husband's name was in the newspaper quite a bit, because of him being in the entertainment business. His nefarious deeds did not make it in there much, thank goodness. One time, in particular, I remember. There was this fete that took place in the wee hours in that upstairs "office" of his tavern on Lowerline Street. There was a coterie of regulars, including Chico and Flyboy and Beanie and Toby. During the bonhomie and so forth, some wag suggested that perhaps, as long as they were up, they'd benefit from some target practice. There were a couple of shotguns handy so they all took turns shooting out the window at the garbage cans in the alley. Especially ole Toby, who had never target shot before but immediately discovered that he liked it a whole lot. They all thought the racket satisfying in its intensity but were dismayed and disappointed that no hue and cry was raised by the neighbors. I guess when you throw your whole heart into being a nuisance it is unsettling if no one even takes note. So that ex-husband, ever resourceful, called the police himself to complain about the noise. The police did come and promptly charged the "office." Whereupon, Toby threw himself upon them with loud cries of "Thank God, you've come! They kidnapped me! You cannot imagine what I have been through!"

The cops searched the office and, along with the weapons,

confiscated two bags of a black substance. Everyone, except Toby, was arrested for kidnapping and possession of a narcotic thought to be hashish.

The *Picayune* condensed all this to one paragraph and used that X's full, legal name—which no one knew. So, fine. I was a nervous wreck because, at the time, I was a student loan officer at a bank and was trying to act normal. To my relief, no one at the bank found out about it, even though charges were actually brought and it went to court. That ex-husband and them were represented by a pair of young lawyers who were regular patrons of the tavern. Toby the victim's family had whined and carried on until this lah-dee-dah friend of theirs agreed to counsel their black sheep. The guy was a senior partner at the biggest law firm in town. So, the D.A. had the two bags of hash and Toby as their star witness. However, he was unavailable for the pre-trial hearing on account of he was in detox.

What the defense side had was the real and actual truth (how lucky!) that the bags of hashish were, in fact, volcanic pumice from that X's mother's trip to Hawaii. This was her idea of a nice souvenir. They also had a box labeled "TOBY TAPES." These were audio tapes—many, many audio tapes. All of them recorded at the tavern. All of them were of Toby "in concert." At the piano, performing his own original material. Now, some of it was quite clever and witty. But every bit of it was just as nasty and foul and gross and obscene as it could be. Yip, *yip, eeeeee.*

The two young lawyers for our side saw to it that all the players huddled for a confab in the judge's chambers. They played just a couple of the choicer "Toby Tapes" for his honor. After which, he said, sternly, "We are going out there and kill this thing and *nobody* better laugh!"

And so, they did. Kill it. No laughter.

Later that same night, at the tavern, that ex-husband happily had his own little concert which included a rendition of "*I fought the law and I won!*"

There was a nice big turnout for the funeral and a huge one for the "wake" afterward at the F&M Patio. Me and my secular advisor Charlie Nelson bemoaned that nobody is going to come to our funerals because we just don't know very many people and some of them are dying and some don't even like us much to start with. We worried about this whenever we happen on a funeral that is well-attended. We have discussed drumming up business for each other's funerals. Since we cannot solve the dilemma of how we would manage to pull this off without one of us getting screwed in the deal, we have been toying with some ideas for evasion tactics. For instance, I thought up the plan that we could put the notice in the paper belatedly. It could say something like: "A private memorial service was held on the Island of Cayman Brac. It was attended by family and very close friends. Among those attending were Prince William of the House of Windsor, Bruce Springsteen, Gore Vidal, several Kennedys, and Bill Gates." Who's gonna know?

We also have had some concerns about that part of the obituary that is like what went next to our pictures in our high school yearbooks. It looks pitiful if you don't have any extra curricular activities. Me and Charlie both wanted a whole lot of activities and honors listed in our obituaries. However, we really did not want to have to join a lotta stuff or do actual activities. And we don't either one of us have any honors.

Our theory is that since the obituary space has to be paid for, whoever is paying decides what goes in there. So, we just need to be sure we get ours written and appoint an agent to see it through. Some of the things we would like in our bios include:

> United States Senator, Ambassador to the Court of St. James, Pulitzer Prize Winner, Peabody Award Winner, Member of Apollo XIII, Three time winner of the Indy 500, Gold medalist in swimming '72 Olympics, author and inspiration for screenplay of "Love Story" and inventor of the Internet.

Some of these are too obviously not our achievements, having been unceremoniously latched onto by others. Only idiots would believe that we had done these things. However, we feel like something less grandiose could fly. Try this on:

> Served as Ad Hoc Judge for the Fifth Circuit from 1982-1984, Member of advisory board for the Chamber of Commerce, Board of Directors for World Bank, Peace Corps

volunteer, maid (or duke) for Krewe of Anthirium, Bronze medallist in dressage. And so on.

Father Bob and Mary Dodwell put on a good funeral for that ex-husband. The Rev paid no mind to the brown dog who was lolling up front and assiduously licking his balls in the devoted way dogs have. He lickedandhelickedandhelickedandhelicked. And he nibbledandnibbled and nibbled. And liiiccckkkked and liiicccckkkked. Finally, I poked him and he sprang up and glared at me, as if to say "What, what?"

Old friends Jim Higgins and Clancy DuBos spoke frankly about their long and often surprising association with the deceased. I would have liked to have said a few words, but I really didn't think I could remain composed enough to do so. Then when Pres Kabacoff got up there for his turn, there was a cloudburst. The rain came pounding down on the copper roof of Bultman's solarium and it was plenty loud. Pres raised his voice—and it rained harder. He started hollering and it rained louder still. There were quite a few chuckles, since many folks there knew that the relationship between that ex-husband and Pres was sometimes adversarial. They figured the timely storm was courtesy of that ex-husband. Pres finally just gave up and sat down. The downpour ceased.

The Rev, on behalf of the nephew, invited all who wished to do so to repair to the F&M to raise a glass to our departed brother.

I wasn't surprised that tons more people came to this part.

It's a lot more fun. The brown dog certainly liked it better, thanks to the funeral nabs of which he enjoyed many. However, it was nothing compared to what we from Mississippi are accustomed to. Perhaps I've been hanging with the wrong folks here in New Orleans, but I just never have run up on any funeral food that would compare to what those Mississippians offer. When my father died, some kind souls brought these Lebanese meat pies that really helped us out. Thank goodness we had the presence of mind to stash them in the car so that our little family could get all of the benefit of the pies. I think that the liquid refreshments have pride of place around in New Orleans. And there's something to be said for that.

There was a nice big turnout for the funeral and the after-gathering at the F&M Patio. The brown dog did not bite a single person and did just a dab of grooming. Thanks to the free pouring sour mash, I maintained a lowgrade snivel for much of the afternoon. Until our old friend Rug, who'd come all the way from Memphis, asked me and my sister did we want to see a trick.

"Ohhhhhh, yes!" we said with one voice, "We just love to see tricks!" The prospect of a trick immediately cheered us.

Beaming with pride, Rug unzipped the black trousers of his funeral outfit and whipped out his member, impaling it with a straw from the bar.

"EWWWWWWW," we squealed, applauding his daring.

Our friend Rug didn't appear to suffer any pain from the trick. I bet he'd done it a thousand times before. In fact, he took several bows before the small crowd that had gathered.

Moviemeister Chappy Hardy caught this and several other things on video that day. Jill remarked to Chappy, "You know from the first time Rug met my sister, he has been wanting to whip out his thang, but he didn't dare to do it while that X was alive. Not even after they split up. Isn't it nice that he waited a decent interval?"

Come See Me Sometime

I DIDN'T SEE THAT EX-HUSBAND AGAIN til about a month after the funeral. I awoke in the middle of the night to find him sitting in the wingback chair next to my bed. He did not glance over at me, instead he kept his eyes dead ahead—so to speak. He looked real good, like he had way before he got sick. He never said a word and I didn't either. I wanted to but I felt too shy. I was consumed with excitement. My heart was racing ninety to nothing. I wanted to phone up somebody to share the news of my first and only "visitation." This was a sure enough supernatural experience. I just didn't know how to act. I'd not run across "Miss Manners' Guide to Receiving the Recently Deceased."

Plus I felt something like a rabbit in tharn. I was paralyzed, but I wasn't afraid. I was excited but I just couldn't will myself to act. I lay there for I-don't-know-how-long, thinking "Say something, idiot!" "Okay, count to three and then talk." "One, two, three, nuthin."

Eventually, I noticed that my heart wasn't pounding anymore. My mind had stopped spinning and counting. I was completely calm and relaxed. The next thing I knew it was morning and he was gone. I still felt elated and certain that this had not been a dream. He had been wearing one of those ugly brown outfits like he'd favored in life. I thought it a little bit of a shame he hadn't gotten better taste in clothes. But he had a nice tan and his hair had been neatly trimmed. And the clincher as far as I was concerned: he'd brought with him the definite aroma of bay rum! In fact, it was still lingering the next morning. Although that ex-husband had often tarried at length and sometimes overnight in that second bachlorette maisonette during life, the atmosphere had certainly not been impregnated with his personal scent.

That was my last olfactory experience, but oftentimes the brown dog would whine and go sniffing room-to-room. I wondered if his bloodhound tendencies enabled him to get whiffs of that X. I vowed to do better, or at least different, at the next encounter. If there ever was one.

There was. About another month passed and my chance came. Same deal. Woke up and there he was in that wingback chair, eyes to the front. Ugly brown outfit. But you know, I couldn't tell you whether it was a *new* outfit or not. I wish I had noticed. If it were, *that* would be fodder for interesting speculation. But, then, so would have his wearing an outfit he'd already owned. This time, I got up out of the bed and stood right in front of him. It seemed like he saw me, or more like he had some notion of my presence, and he stood up too. If he'd been breathing I could have felt it on my face. But I didn't. I wanted to give him a hug, but thought that probably my hands would go right through him. Like Casper. I knew he'd be terribly embarrassed to find himself totally without substance. So, I tentatively and cautiously moved my hands closer, closer to him. Then I very gently placed my hands on his forearms, which were hanging down by his sides. I found solid ground! He was (as they say) "like, real!" How thrilling this was. And what a relief. I ran my hands up his arms, across his shoulders and around this neck. My feet knew to slide and take their place between his. His arms were around me, his hands crossed on the small of my back. We moved as close together as we could and held each other. I felt a warmth from the inside as well as from him. My heart just swelled with the sweetness of it. It was the most fulfilling embrace I've ever been a part of. I felt completely comforted and cared for. I was able to give myself over and trust in the moment in a way I'd never been able to quite manage in life. It was altogether special. Except logistically speaking—in that way it seemed just about like our normal hug. Just about. I drew back, realizing what the subtle difference was. "You're so much taller," I squeaked. "About five or six inches taller!"

"Yes," he smiled smugly, "That's one of the perks!"

In real life, he was already 6' 2". But for him more had always been better. I wondered what other enhancements he'd taken advantage of.

We stood there for some while, grinning foolishly and then he was gone. I couldn't tell you if he went in a flash or a fadeout. It was just that, at some particular moment, I became aware that he was no longer there. It was really odd. So was my realization that he had talked without moving his lips. Ventriloquism? I think I heard his thoughts. Big deal, we could sometimes do that in real life.

He would return many times for fleeting visits. But, no more chatting. I was just furious that I had used my one chance to speak with someone from the other side to talk about their height! There were tons of things I wanted to ask. Like: "How's my Daddy?" or at least "Have you seen Elvis?" "Is it crowded?" "Are there lines?" and "Did you get in any trouble for being such an asshole?"

New Arrival

T IME PASSED. About four years worth. That nephew had grown taller and stronger and wiser. He had moved back in with me for a short while after that ex-husband's funeral. As he took over that ex-husband's business affairs, he found his own apartment again. He shared it with his old and best friend Marcos.

The brown dog grew crabbier and crabbier and eventually became really unfit for proper company. There just wasn't enough liability insurance in the world. But he lived a really long time. That's all you need to know. I cannot even think about dead dogs without squalling. So, let's just say that the brown dog relocated and leave it at that. I'm telling this and that's how this part's gonna go.

One day that nephew was over at the F&M Patio Bar, watching Lolly the Day Manager give grief to delivery guys.

Who should come slinking, skulking, sidling through the back door, in search of bar food remnants: BROWN DOG, JUNIOR. I'm not kidding. It was a little brown dog. The spitting image of *the* brown dog. Identical in every way, except younger and about 30% smaller. A bit of research revealed that he'd been hanging around the F&M at night for about two months. He'd honed his begging skills and had become quite the little whore-dog, pandering boldly to all comers for cheese fries. But when the quest for food wasn't involved, he was mighty skittish and scared. Somebody had been mistreating this dog. But it hadn't made him a bit mean. He was just as sweet and loving as the brown dog was cranky. Not that the brown dog wasn't sweet and loving toward us. He was only mean to other people.

Despite brown dog junior's ever so gentle and polite demeanor, he was thought by many of the bar rabble to be the reincarnation of that ex-husband, come back to check things out. Maybe he *had* become what I'd always claimed he was: a hairy hound from hell.

You know, I've never been one who cared much for the reincarnation theory. The notion just doesn't appeal to me in the least. To me, if you're unaware of all your lives, past and future, well, who gives a rat's ass. Like I always say, "If I don't know about it, it didn't happen." By the way, this was one of the things that ex-husband really liked about me.

Anyway, that nephew took to the new brown dog right off. In about a week they were a team. Soon after, brown dog jr.

came to spend the night at my house. That first morning I opened my eyes to spy him standing up in the bed, right by my face. I stared at his arm and thought, "This looks really familiar, where have I seen this arm before?"

And then, the hair on the back of my neck stood up and, as we say in the South, I got chillbumps. Brown dog jr.'s arms were just exactly like that ex-husband's. All angular and sinewy and kind of flat. Of course, that ex-husband's arms had not been covered with fur. But he had those funny, crusty calluses on his elbows, just like this brown dog. What a coincidence.

Kindred spirits now, that nephew and the little brown dog began going most everywhere together, just as that ex-husband and the brown dog had. The little brown dog was quite the furball—constantly shedding golden brown hairs everywhere. One time after that nephew and the little brown dog had spent the whole morning in the car together, they made a stop at Walgreen's at the Riverside shopping center. The little brown dog remained in the car—with all windows all the way down as always. He was already far too precious for us to risk having him wind up as baked dog. That nephew was halfway to the door when he noticed that his clothing was so covered in dog hair, he looked like a man in a dogsuit. He fell to brushing and scraping and slapping and shaking all about in order to rid himself of the furry coating. Shortly, he was the epicenter of a large cloud of golden brown dog hairs. He continued on inside, leaving the cloud behind him, near the store entrance. He was as impervious as the two women lost in a chat who came up behind him. They failed to notice the hairy obstacle right in their path and marched straight into the maelstrom. They also failed to hold their breath and immediately sucked down lungfuls of doghair. Much coughing and snorting and eye-watering followed. I was in the car too, so I got to watch. It was very amusing. I covered my mouth so the ladies wouldn't hear me laughing at them.

One thing that helps out a bit with the dog hair problem is to put something on the dog to contain it. We thought about keeping him in a sack, head sticking out, tied shut with a bow around the neck. He wouldn't like that much. What we found that he did like was a little black leather Harley Davidson motorcycle jacket. Kid size, complete with all the little zippered pockets and everything. He loved to wear it. He was proud, you could tell. He held his head up higher, but would look down every now and then to admire how nice his arms looked covered by leather sleeves. The little brown dog looked so precious that we got a new saying hereabouts: "That's cuter than a little brown dog in a motorcycle jacket!"

After finishing up at Walgreen's, we drove down Tchoupitoulas street to the F&M so that nephew could meet up with his good friend Juan Carlos de Cabaza (in English, this means "Upside down"). He was from Cozumel, Mexico, visiting for business reasons. Juan Carlos got to meet me and the little brown dog for the first time. While we were doing that, the claw machine guy came by on his regular rounds. He had a big sack of prizes to add to the claw machine. He said hello to me and then turned to that nephew. "Hey," he said, "Who's your little brown friend?"

That nephew was taken aback by this blunt and rude inquiry, but he answered, "Oh, this is my friend Juan Carlos from Cozumel."

Sez claw machine guy with a smirk, "Well, that's nice, but I was talking about your dog."

After the guy left, that nephew was all over Juan Carlos apologizing for his mistake. Juan Carlos laughed and said, "That's all right, man, I thought he was talking about me too!"

About a week later, I got a craving for Chinese food. "So what?" you ask. Well, I hadn't eaten or wanted to eat any Chinese food for years because I'd eaten it nearly every Sunday night of my entire married life. That X was crazy about it and would cut up so if he didn't get his weekly ration of "Sub gum woo woo," as he so wittily liked to call his favorite dish. For years we'd been regulars at the Cantonese Restaurant, even before they built the big one off Clearview in Metairie. We started with them when they were in this tacky strip mall on Jefferson Highway.

I gave in to my craving and took myself to the late Maple Gardens Restaurant on Maple Street, which was a favorite of that nephew. I gleefully banged down a couple of Wan Fus, which is Chinese for Chardonnay, followed by spring rolls, rumaki and chow fun. I couldn't believe how much I enjoyed it. I saved most of the rumaki for the little brown dog. I had forgotten that I hate rumaki. I love the way it looks. But the rest was really a treat. I guess my resentment of Chinese food was gone, along with that ex-husband. The best part, however, was the fortune cookie. I broke it apart and read, with interest:

ANCIENT CHINESE PROVERB SAYS: MAN WHO IS FAITHLESS IN LIFE SHALL COME BACK AS A DOG.

And so he has.

Hmmmm. "Is this a karmic message?" I asked myself. Who knows. Who cares.

I'll tell you the kind of karmic stuff I enjoy. It's like this: That nephew took over that ex-husband's business affairs. This meant great piles of papers to deal with. That X never in his life threw anything away. Among the piles of papers were some pertaining to life insurance. That nephew told me that that X had kept me as a beneficiary, even after all those years. I was so tickled. Not just about the money, which I did like. I was also tickled at the thoughtiness. What a nice gesture. I wondered if it was an oversight. That he'd just forgotten to take my name off the policy. People do that all the time. Their lives and the people in them change, but they forget to change the paperwork. But this was not the case here. The insurance guy told me that they reviewed all that stuff every year. And every year, that ex-husband would say that he didn't want to change anything. He had done it on purpose!

Whereupon I began to feel more warmly toward that X than I had even in real life. I no longer thought of him as "That Asshole." I no longer even thought of him as "That Ex-

Husband." I lovingly bestowed upon him an immediate up-grade. Henceforth and forevermore, he was indeed "MY-LATE-HUSBAND-BLESS-HIS-HEART!"

Acknowledgements

I'm very grateful to my publisher, editor and adviser, Joshua Clark—the man knows how to couch his criticism. To Malcolm White for encouraging me to write for his Jackson, Mississippi paper, *The Diddy Wah Diddy*. To Marda Burton for her faith and help. Her Sunday salons were a creative outlet for me and countless others. To Rosemary James for including some of my Brown Dog stories in the Faulkner Society Magazine, *Double Dealer Redux*. Peter Mayer, Frank Montagnino and Fred Baldwin were the very first ones to read what I wrote and laugh. To my secular advisers, Charles Nelson, Kyle Jennings and Marshall Page. And to Jeanie Clinton for all her help, and having some of the best friends on this Earth.

My thanks to friends Carol Gremillion Mitchell, Sharon Frederick, Susan Sanford, Angela Comfort and Lisa Hendricks for giving me the chance to do my twenties over again.

And thanks to Hens: Nell Carmichael, Sandra Querbes, Nora Fine, Sandy Cason, Ellen Harris, Sue Meyer and the late Dorothy Blackwood.

And to friends Sharon Rowe Johnson, Bonnie Broome, Sharol David, Joe Buttram, Marcus Barnett, Barbara Cunningham Agent, Terry McGuckin, Jane Lawton, Cynthia Cashman and Ellen Dollacker.

And to a matchless crew: Diane Riche, Randi de la Gueronniere and Armide de la Gueronniere.

To Trevor, Ruth Anna, Riley and Bailey for providing solace and support.

My late father passed along his sense of humor and my mother read to me until she was blue in the face.

My thanks to my sister Jill for being my spiritual twin. And for her generous helping heart.

And, lastly, my gratitude to Otis and Chester and all the wonderful brown dogs of the world.

About the Author

A Renaissance woman, the author is passionate about many things, certainly all the arts and most of the sciences. Her special interest is classical dressage, although she does not compete. Her proudest possession is her Hermes dressure saddle. International affairs have long been of interest and lead to her involvement with the League for Standardization and Transparency (seeking to make everything just alike and see-through) and the World Ennui Society (for the preservation of the endangered ennui). Further, this provided her opportunity to keep fluent in her five languages. Her prize-winning roses and camellias delight the many visitors to her home, "The Snuggery." But what pleases her friends most are the treasures she bestows at Christmas. Last year she handknit angora sweaters and scarves for her twenty closest. They were concealed in handblocked wrapping paper designed by the author. Each was accompanied by cards with individual watercolors and messages in her beautifully executed calligraphy. Her wide-ranging interests and expertise bring her to the judging table for a host of shows and competitions involving art, ballet, opera and things equestrian. And, by the way, her ass is a Chinese typewriter and she's double-jointed.

Come say hi:

<u>www.southernfrieddivorce.com</u>

This book is available nationwide
at your favorite bookseller.

For more from Light of New Orleans Publishing see also

<u>www.frenchquarterfiction.com</u>